CONSULTING with the ENNEAGRAM

BODY

6. Closing

5. Changing

9

8   1

7   2

1. Contracting

4. Challenging

6   3

5   4

HEAD

HEART

2. Collecting

3. Communicating

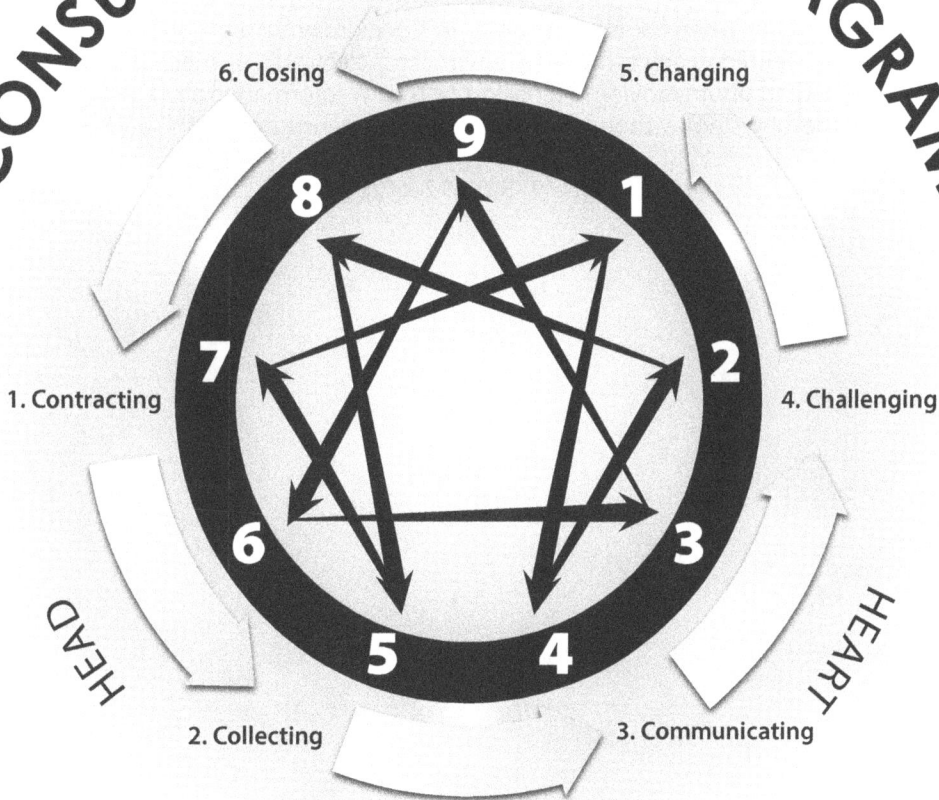

Ginger Lapid-Bogda, Ph.D.

The Enneagram In Business Press | Santa Monica, California

Consulting with the Enneagram

ISBN: 978-0-692-41269-5

The Enneagram In Business Press
Santa Monica, California
310.829.3309

www.TheEnneagramInBusiness.com

TABLE of CONTENTS | CONSULTING with THE ENNEAGRAM

INTRODUCTION	1
CHAPTER 1 | ENNEAGRAM	3
CHAPTER 2 | FOUNDATIONS	25
CHAPTER 3 | CONTRACTING	41
CHAPTER 4 | COLLECTING	55
CHAPTER 5 | COMMUNICATING	69
CHAPTER 6 | CHALLENGING	91
CHAPTER 7 | CHANGING	101
CHAPTER 8 | CLOSING	125
CHAPTER 9 | CONSULTANT DEVELOPMENT	133
CHAPTER 10 | CASE STUDIES	141
CHAPTER 11 | ACTIVITIES	161
APPENDIX	175
BIBLIOGRAPHY	187
ABOUT THE AUTHOR	190

INTRODUCTION | CONSULTING with THE ENNEAGRAM

I am very excited about this book, one that covers how to consult to organizations using the Enneagram. In it you will find a 6-step consulting process fully integrated with the insights of the Enneagram. Throughout my 40 plus years of consulting, I have always heard, believed, and followed this phrase: *Trust the process*. Why? Because consulting is different from coaching, where we work 1-1 with a coaching client, and it is also different from training, where we agree to teach a certain body of subject matter to a specific group, and we, the trainer, go in knowing pretty much what will be covered, how it will be covered, and what we can expect along the way. We are training concepts, skills, attitudes and more. But we pretty much know what will happen before we begin.

Consulting is entirely different. It requires a more rigorous skill set, greater diagnostic skills, and we are dealing with the client's real issues in real time. As a result, the risk is higher for the client and the stakes are higher for the consultant. Much that emerges in real time requires adjustments, big and small. The consultant must really know what he or she is doing or they can actually cause great damage to the organization and to the people with whom they work. Consultants can also add enormous value to organizations, transforming the organization and the people within it, far more than coaching or training, although all have value.

As a result, *trust the process* is essential to successful consulting, but the process must be one you can actually trust. That 6-step process is in this book, easy to follow, rigorous, time-tested. Whether you are new to consulting or an old-timer, you still need to follow the process. Does this mean all your consulting efforts will be successful? No, but most of them will be and you will learn from experience, getting better and better as you do.

Why the Enneagram integrated with the consulting process and consulting skills? You can be a really good consultant without the Enneagram, but with the Enneagram, your consulting can move from good to great. You can actually customize each step of the process to your client's Enneagram type, increasing the impact of whatever you do. And you can work on your own development as a consultant using the Enneagram, as described in the later part of this book.

This book is the outcome of many factors and sources. First, almost all the consulting technologies included have their source in the work of NTL (National Training Labs), an internationally known organization that is over 50 years old and gave birth to the field of OD (Organizational Development). As a NTL member for 25 years, NTL has been fundamental in my professional background. I've taught T-groups (human interaction labs) for even longer than I've been a NTL member. For NTL, I've taught T-groups, consulting skills, intervention skills, and change management. I've also taught intensive consulting skills programs for Arthur Andersen Business Consulting, for the US Postal Service, for Antioch University, UCLA, and Sonoma State University. This is all in addition to my own experience as an OD consultant, where I have been known as "a consultant who does not cut corners." I follow and trust the process and get excellent results almost every time.

When the Enneagram found me – yes, the Enneagram has a way of finding people, which is why it is "sticky" – 20 years ago, I began integrating it into all my consulting projects, getting better and faster results for clients at half the cost to them, even though my consulting fees have gone up in 20 years.

So if you are already an OD consultant, but have not been using the Enneagram in your work, this book will help you do that. The early chapter on the Enneagram will help you with the system and the 9 types, as will information in the Appendix on more aspects of the Enneagram such as wings, arrows, and subtypes.

If you are a trainer who already uses the Enneagram, this book can help you in two ways. First, if you have a long-term training engagement with a client, there are aspects of the 6-step consulting model that will help you greatly improve what you train and how you design your training. This book can also help you expand your offerings to include consulting and to know which will better fit your client's needs, training or consulting.

If you are an Enneagram-based coach who wants to consult with your clients, this book can show you the methodology, which is entirely different from coaching 1-1. I've seen many coaches venture into working with the teams of their clients, only to be unsuccessful because they had neither a consulting approach, nor diagnostic skills, and didn't understand team dynamics or organizational structure and processes. This book can help with all that.

A thank you to all my consulting clients over the years at organizations such as Sun Microsystems, GE, Apple, Clorox, TRW, Disney, Genentech/Roche, Kaiser Permanente, Salesforce, P & G and more. I have learned more on the job than I ever learned from books and training, but without the books and training, I would never have known what to do, why it works, and how to make my consulting better and better.

And a special thank you to my dear friend and colleague, Pat Bidol Padva. This book has its roots in my "Consulting with the Enneagram" 5-day program, and Pat, who learned the Enneagram in the early days of OD from her mentor, Ron Lippitt, helped me design my first program. In "Consulting with the Enneagram," participants engage in a rigorous process of consulting with real clients, and the results are masterful.

And a thank you to my Enneagram inspirers: Claudio Naranjo, Helen Palmer, Don Riso, and David Daniels. Without them, none of my Enneagram books would exist, nor would the contemporary Enneagram, as we know it, be possible.

CHAPTER 1
ENNEAGRAM | CONSULTING with THE ENNEAGRAM

The Enneagram is a psychological and spiritual system that goes beyond the personality into a deep and powerful description of the human character, specifically the 9 structures of the ego. The Enneagram's Asian and Middle Eastern roots are ancient, and at its foundation is the Eastern philosophy and practice of self-observation.

The word itself comes from the Greek words ennea ("nine") and gram ("something written or drawn"), referring to the nine points on the Enneagram symbol. These nine different Enneagram types or points reflect 9 distinct patterns of thinking, feeling, and behaving, with each type connected to a specific and unique path of development.

A person's Enneagram type appears early in childhood and does not change over time, although individuals of the same type may behave quite differently based on a number of factors: level of self-mastery; use of wings – the types on either side of a person's core Enneagram type; use of arrow lines – the arrow lines pointing toward and away from the individual's core type; and subtypes, the three different versions of each type. More information about these additional factors can be found in the appendix of this book.

The Enneagram's ancient history is uncertain, although the system first appeared in both Asia and the Middle East several thousand years ago or longer. Because the Enneagram evolved as an oral tradition, it is difficult to know its exact origins. In the 20th century, three individuals brought the Enneagram into modern usage: G.I. Gurdjieff in the 1930s in Europe; Oscar Ichazo in the 1950s in South America; and Claudio Naranjo, a Chilean-born American psychiatrist, who studied with Ichazo, then brought the system to the United States the 1970s.

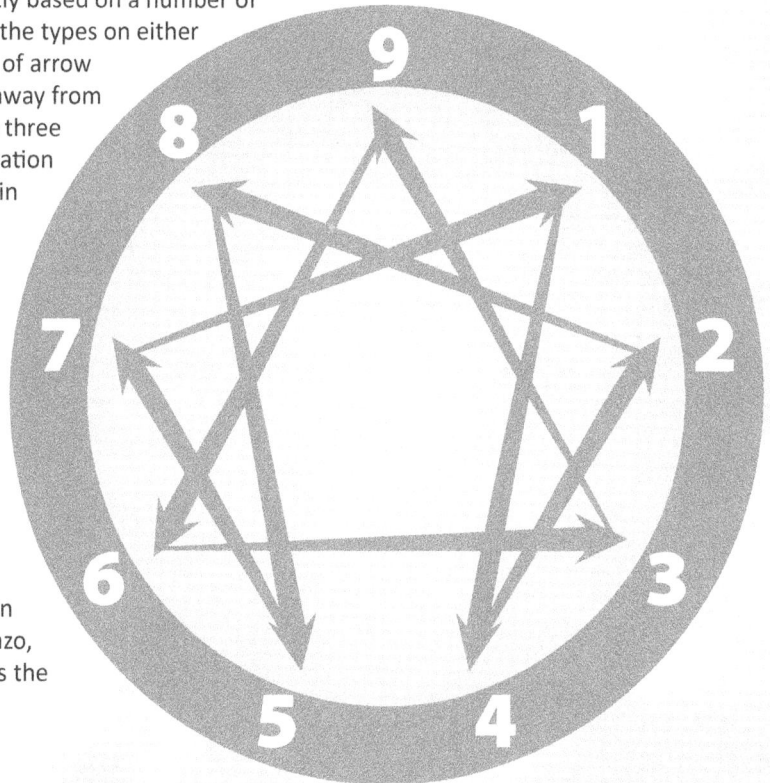

The 9 Enneagram Types | Enneagram Ones

The Perfectionist

ONES seek a perfect world and work diligently to improve both themselves and everyone and everything around them.

Perfectionists (ONES) search for perfection and avoid making mistakes. Symbolized by this simple and elegant tree, Ones are rooted and grounded, upright in a variety of ways, and they are also prudent and self-contained, more structured than flexible, and honest yet polite.

Discerning and judging, quality-focused and responsible, highly organized and easily resentful, Enneagram Ones structure their worlds and exert self-control in order to ensure that they, others around them, and their environments align as closely as possible to their refined and precise ideals and standards of excellence. Ones don't really believe that true perfection is possible, but they do believe what matters most is that people are constantly working on improvement toward these ideals.

All Ones have an internalized set of high standards, a long set of expectations about how they and others should behave, and have an instinctive and quick response about how activities should be both structured and executed. All Ones, however, do not necessarily share the same exact standards. In addition, some Ones worry in advance about meeting their own standards and getting everything right; other Ones perceive themselves as closer to perfect than the rest of us and view themselves as role models of excellence; and still other Ones direct their standards of perfection to others by constantly trying to improve them!

The One's interpersonal style is normally clear, precise, direct, and exacting, using carefully chosen words and phrases expressed in a seemingly polite manner. They are both self-controlled and spontaneously reactive, amused and skeptical, playful yet decidedly serious, and gracious, yet prone to flares of irritation or outbursts of anger, which they prefer to call frustration.

Worldview | The world is imperfect; I must correct this.

Beliefs | "If something's not worth doing right, it's not worth doing; no one is perfect, but what matters most is improvement."

Motivation | being as perfect and self-controlled as possible

Avoidance | making mistakes, being incorrect, or showing anger directly

Likes | excellence - self-improvement - talent

Dislikes | impolite behavior - errors of all kinds - mediocrity

Growth areas | Ones can be highly self-critical as well as critical or judging of others, particularly when things don't go well. They can be very hard on themselves, being especially sensitive to feeling criticized by other people. They are strongly opinionated and become easily irritated and resentful when things are not right. In their effort to avoid mistakes, they can be controlling and overly detail-focused. They also find it hard to relax unless away from the pressures of daily life. Although they try hard not to show it when they feel angry or upset, others can usually sense the One's displeasure. However, through targeted development work on these specific growth areas, Ones can achieve their deepest longing.

Deepest longing | experiencing a serene life and accepting the world as it is

The Friend

TWOS want to be liked, try to meet the needs of others, and attempt to orchestrate the people and events in their lives.

Friends (TWOS) search for appreciation and avoid feeling unworthy. Symbolized by this gift that Twos continuously want to offer others, the gifts that Twos give contain something the Two believes the other person wants or needs: attention, resources, time, an object the other person admired, a poem or a kind word, advice, or even a surprise.

Optimistic, generous, and empathic, Enneagram Twos focus on the needs and behavior of others far more than on their own needs and desires; they develop an intuitive ability to know how to best support others in achieving their dreams or in minimizing their suffering. Although Twos do want people to like them, it can be misleading to think that all Twos want everyone with whom they come in contact with to like them. A more accurate understanding is that Twos want, and even expect, the people they want to like them to respond favorably, but care far less — if at all — whether people they dislike find them appealing. What is true of almost all Twos is that they can become extremely distressed when someone whose opinion or affection they care about perceives them in a negative way.

Most Twos appear warm, are good listeners, and offer advice that they hope and expect others will take. Some Twos appear vulnerable, even childlike as if needing protection; other Twos exhibit more assertiveness, focusing their efforts to help or move groups or institutions in a forward direction; and still other Twos derive their sense of value and importance by being desirable and indispensible to special individuals in their lives.

Twos tend to engage with others in a consistently warm way, usually asking questions of others more often than talking about themselves. While most Twos have well-developed interpersonal skills, they can also become self-effacing and uncomfortable when the focus is primarily on them.

Worldview | The world is full of suffering and need; I must help alleviate this.

Beliefs | "Relationships are what matter most; you can know what others need if you just pay close attention."

Motivation | developing relationships in which they help other people in an implicit exchange for the others' gratitude

Avoidance | feeling needy or unworthy

Likes | generosity - making a difference in people's lives - kindness

Dislikes | being taken for granted - others being treated abusively - thoughtlessness

Growth areas | Their continuous focus on other people causes Twos to pay little attention to what they themselves feel, need, and want. The result is Twos have difficulty saying *no* when others ask for assistance, feel deeply depleted at times, become distressed when others don't also offer to support in return, and become resentful when their "good works" go unappreciated or misinterpreted. In addition, people with whom Twos were once close may distance themselves because they either felt overly dependent on the Two or perceived the Two's generosity as a way for the Two to indirectly make themselves feel worthy or valued. However, through targeted development work on these specific growth areas, Twos can achieve their deepest longing.

Deepest longing | feeling a deep and firm sense of self-worth that is not dependent on how others respond to them

The Performer

THREES organize their lives around achieving specific goals in order to appear successful and to gain the respect and admiration of others.

Performers (THREES) search for success and avoid failure at all costs. Symbolized by the target, Threes take steady aim at their goals, develop a plan for hitting the bull's eye, and then do everything they can to hit their mark.

High energy, confident, and achievement oriented, Enneagram Threes focus on results they believe will bring them the respect of others and on efficient and effective plans for accomplishing these goals. As a result, they create a persona of confidence and success, but often at the expense of being completely genuine. They lose touch with both their deeper feelings and a true sense of who they really are, often confusing their "public" image with their real selves.

Although all Threes share a success orientation and constant need to have goals and plans, there are also differences among them. Some Threes are highly self-reliant, strive to be the model of a "good" person, and create an image of being authentic and having no image; other Threes create an image of being high status, having prestige, and being important as a result of their ability to perform and their credentials, position, and high-influence friends; and some Threes focus more on creating an image of being extremely attractive in a highly masculine or feminine way, having less need for visibility and a greater desire to support the success of important people in their lives.

The Three's interpersonal style is one of having strong, deliberate, and confident stage presence. They convey their ideas in a well-conceived and highly self-assured way, have strong social skills except when they are stressed — at which times they can be cold and abrupt — and often appear as if they were born to give public presentations.

Worldview | There is a lack of flow and order to how things work: I must organize and plan to get results.

Beliefs | "The world values a winner and ignores or ridicules losers; stay focused on your goals and plans, then everything falls into place."

Motivation | being successful, getting results, and gaining respect

Avoidance | not failing at anything they do

Likes | efficiency - effectiveness - achievement

Dislikes | unproductive people - being treated as if they are a nobody - doing nothing

Growth areas | Their strong focus on activities, tasks, and achieving goals causes Threes to become over-extended, with limited time for deeper personal relationships, self-reflection, or exploring their feelings in depth. Threes become frustrated and impatient when obstacles arise, and they act curt or even harsh with others when they are tense or anxious. When strong feelings emerge – in either the Three or other people – Threes prefer to not discuss the issues at length; they may change the subject, engage in activities that distract them, or make it clear to others that they don't want to talk for very long or very deeply. However, through targeted development work on these specific growth areas, Threes can achieve their deepest longing.

Deepest longing | knowing who they really are and to be valued by both themselves and others for who they are, not just for what they accomplish

The 9 Enneagram Types | Enneagram Fours

The Unique One

FOURS desire deep connections with both their own interior worlds and with other people, and feel most alive when they authentically express their personal experiences and feelings.

Unique Ones (FOURS) search for deep experiences and emotional connection and avoid rejection and feeling not good enough. Symbolized by the jigsaw puzzle piece, Fours perceive themselves as a puzzle, trying to figure out why they feel so different from others and what makes them unique. To this end, they consciously and unconsciously compare themselves to others, and as a result, Fours either end up feeling superior, inferior or both.

Individualistic, emotionally sensitive, and creative, Fours seek deep meaning, authentic connections, and they tend to idealize that which seems unavailable, being especially attuned to what is missing in their complex worlds. Focusing on their internal experiences as a way of understanding and finding meaning, Fours seek to be deeply understood and want to be perceived as unique, special, or different.

Although all Fours have a special connection to suffering and have robust, complex inner lives full of nuance and symbolism, some Fours are hyper-active and risk-taking, silently enduring their suffering as a badge of virtue; other Fours are hyper-sensitive and more despairing, wanting to be accepted unconditionally for who they are; and still other Fours exhibit a flair for the dramatic and engage in extreme competition with others in hopes of winning and taking center-stage, thus minimizing their sense of not being good enough.

The Four's interpersonal style combines an abundance of self-referencing speech — that is, the extensive use of words such as *I*, *me*, *my*, and *mine* as well as personal stories — and they often use emotion-laden and metaphoric language. It is as if their own inner worlds are the center of the universe, or at least, the center of their universe.

Worldview | There is profound despair that comes from our lack of deep connectedness: I must re-establish these.

Beliefs | "Nothing has meaning nor can be fully understood unless you go deeply into your own personal experience; joy and suffering are part of being human."

Motivation | experiencing the most profound aspects of life through an intense level of connectedness with self and others

Avoidance | living superficially or feeling deficient

Likes | meaningful conversations - authentic self-expression - feeling understood

Dislikes | not knowing what they are searching for or missing - being ignored or slighted - someone breaking off a connection before they are ready

Growth areas | Because Fours think of themselves as unique, special, and different, they are concerned with what makes them different. They compare themselves to others regularly and sometimes concluding that they are superior, sometimes deciding that there is something wrong with them, and at other times, they don't know what to think. Their strong desire to be understood is a way in which they feel connected to others, but this gets complicated because their interior life is constantly shifting. Fours are highly sensitive to rejection, can be moody, and become easily bored with the ordinariness of life. However, through targeted development work on these specific growth areas, Fours can achieve their deepest longing.

Deepest longing | living a deep, purposeful, and emotionally balanced life

The Expert

FIVES thirst for knowledge and use emotional detachment as a way of keeping involvement with others at a minimum.

Experts (FIVES) search for knowledge and wisdom and avoid intrusion and loss of energy. Symbolized by the light bulb representing mental knowledge, Fives try to accumulate information from which they can gain insight and wisdom.

Emotionally detached, private, self-controlled, and highly independent — autonomous may be a more accurate description — Fives have an insatiable need to know, particularly about areas that interest or concern them. Fully understanding how everything works and fits together helps Fives believe that they are on the path to wisdom, but just as important, accumulating knowledge helps them feel prepared for the inevitable surprises they would prefer not to experience. The quest for privacy is a constant among Fives, although the areas they consider private vary widely. Some Fives like to share their knowledge, while others consider this proprietary. Some Fives are highly private about what they do in their spare time, while others consider their age, marital status, and other such personal information to be in the confidential realm.

All Fives automatically detach from their feelings in the actual moment of an emotional experience, reactivating some of these feelings later, at a more convenient and private time. Fives also compartmentalize or isolate aspects of their lives from other parts. However, the content of what Fives compartmentalize can differ widely. Some Fives compartmentalize their work life from their home life; others keep their friends separated from one another; and other Fives keep themselves isolated from other people. However, all Fives separate their minds from their emotions, their emotions from their bodies, and their bodies from their minds.

In addition, most Fives are extremely wary of intrusions on their physical space, their time and energy, and demands for intense interpersonal interactions. Some Fives keep extremely controlled boundaries and are attached to their seclusion, coming out for more engagement at specifically selected moments; other Fives are more outgoing and social — though the content of their conversations tends to be information and facts that interest them — and are so drawn to lofty ideals that they can lose interest in everyday life; and some Fives engage primarily with the few others they completely trust and with whom they feel a special bond.

The Five's interpersonal style is highly self-contained, with little animation in either their voice tone, body language or both. They may appear forthcoming about giving information and others less so, but all Fives appear remote to some degree. Some Fives may be engaging in a way that attracts others and others less so, but all Fives make it obvious that there are clear boundaries about what they will discuss and how they will discuss it.

Worldview | Resources are scarce: I must conserve my time, energy, and knowledge or I will be entirely depleted.

Beliefs | "Everything is potentially knowable; the mind is the only thing you can trust."

Motivation | accumulating knowledge and preserving their autonomy

Avoidance | not loosing energy by having others intrude on them

Likes | competence - information - personal privacy and space

Dislikes | intrusion - ignorance - emotionality

Growth areas | Because Fives automatically detach from their emotions, keep their needs to a minimum, and rely solely on themselves, they can feel isolated and disconnected from other people. It takes them a very long time to trust others, and this trust can be easily broken should the other person let them down. When they do interact with people, Fives have very mixed feelings about this and can come across as aloof and remote. Although Fives often have many talents and interests, others do not know this about them since they keep this information to themselves. However, through targeted development work on these specific growth areas, Fives can achieve their deepest longing.

Deepest longing | experiencing and fully understanding life at all levels – mental, emotional and physical

The 9 Enneagram Types | Enneagram Sixes

The Questioner

SIXES have insightful minds and create anticipatory or worst-case scenarios to help themselves feel prepared in case something goes wrong. Some are tentative, some engage in high-risk behavior to prove their fearlessness, and some do both.

Questioners (SIXES) search for meaning, certainty, and trust and avoid negative scenarios from occurring. Symbolized by the question mark inside the mind, Sixes question everything as a way to feel prepared for every contingency.

Sharp-minded, insightful, and loyal, Sixes are issue identifiers and problem solvers, with a mental-emotional antenna that is finely attuned to anticipate problems before they occur so that alternative paths and contingency plans can be created. This is done to ensure the best possible outcome and prevent the worst from happening. Although the above description applies to all Sixes, Sixes are complex individuals who run the gamut from phobic Sixes, who are overtly and palpably fearful, to counter-phobic Sixes, who often mask their fear by taking dramatic risks — often, but not always, physical ones — that adrenalize them and prove to themselves and others, at least for the moment, that they are not fearful. Many Sixes display characteristics of the phobic and the counter-phobic Six.

All Sixes worry as a habit of mind, although some Sixes call it instantaneous anticipatory planning or problem solving, and other Sixes do this so naturally that they no longer notice it. There are also key differences among Sixes. Some Sixes deal with their concerns by becoming warm, inviting, and by developing strong and loyal social alliances as a way to feel safe; other Sixes become extraordinarily dutiful and try to know and adhere to the "rules" as a way to not get in trouble by going astray; and still other Sixes — the highly counter-phobic Sixes — unconsciously turn against their fear with demonstrations of strength as a way to convince themselves and others of their bravery. In reality, most phobic Sixes have some counter-phobic qualities — for example, they can become aggressive toward authority or authority figures — and most counter-phobic Sixes do share their fears and concerns with those they trust or demonstrate it through their non-verbal behavior.

Sixes have a variety of interpersonal styles, but most are warm; loyal; appear genuine, displaying a relative lack of pretentiousness; candid; agile in expressing concerns; and willing to talk truthfully about themselves.

Worldview | The world is an unstable, unpredictable, and dangerous place; I must find meaning and certainty.

Beliefs | "Hope for the best, plan for the worst; dutiful and loyal people like me can be counted on, and this may prevent negative things from happening."

Motivation | finding certainty, support, and loyalty

Avoidance | negative scenarios and feeling anxious and fearful

Likes | loyalty - risk management - problem solving

Dislikes | unpredictable or unjust authorities - someone saying to them, "You are imagining things" - untrustworthy behavior

Growth areas | Sixes are overly compliant, overly defiant, or both, especially when it comes to dealing with authority figures. Sixes may avoid, befriend, or battle authorities, or engage in all three behaviors at different times. Although they like risk, they don't like ambiguity, a difficult balance because with risk there is always some ambiguity. When they worry and feel doubtful, they project their concerns onto others, but at the same time, also doubt their own perceptions and abilities. If there is too much uncertainty, Sixes become immobilized; if there is too much certainty, they become bored. A more tentative Six – the phobic Six – often takes few risks in life; a more assertive – the counter-phobic – Six engages in dangerous activities to adrenalize themselves, living life on the edge. Some Sixes do both. All of this makes Sixes very complex. However, through targeted development work on these specific growth areas, Sixes can achieve their deepest longing.

Deepest longing | being able to fully trust themselves, others, and their environment

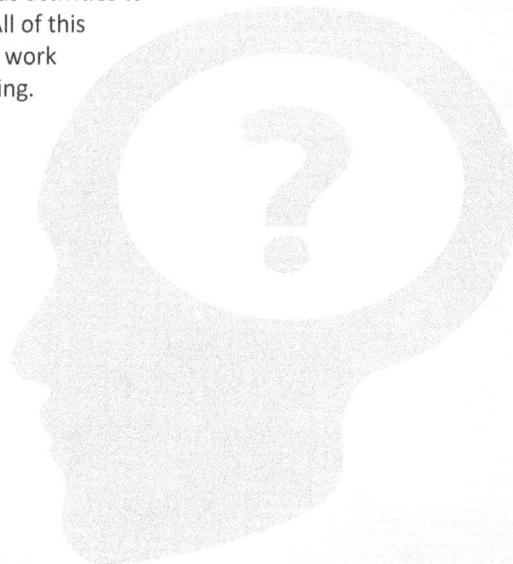

The 9 Enneagram Types | Enneagram Sevens

The Energizer

SEVENS crave the stimulation of new ideas, people, and experiences, avoid pain and discomfort, and engage in positive possibility planning, thus allowing them to keep all of their options open.

Energizers (SEVENS) search for pleasure and stimulation and avoid pain and discomfort. Symbolized by the glass of champagne, Sevens are bubbly and effervescent, trying to enjoy life's pleasures and positive possibilities.

Spontaneous, engaging, and multitasking to an extreme, Sevens are upbeat, energetic, and need to feel that they have all options possible open to them. Elaborate future planners, dreamers and visionaries, Sevens generate enthusiasm, push boundaries, and avoid painful experiences by conjuring up new ideas, engaging with people or activities that excite them, and by rationalizing negative experiences through a positive reframing of events.

Almost all Sevens have difficulty focusing on one thing at a time, as their attention shifts from one idea, activity, or person to the next thing that grabs their interest, and they also have a contagious sense of optimism that comes from a sense that everything is possible. Some Sevens create extensive social networks, a kind of collective surrogate family that gives them the support to make the best of every opportunity; other Sevens temporarily restrain their desire to have everything as a way to sacrifice themselves in the service of the group; and still other Sevens are unabashed dreamers, looking to everything new to stimulate and excite them. For Sevens like this, their "dream" is often far better than reality.

Their interpersonal style can be described as fast-talking and even faster thinking, with a mental process that moves 1000 miles per hour and jumps from topic to topic. While some Sevens are quiet, most Sevens say what's on their minds as soon as they think it. And although their ideas may seem loosely connected to the rest of us, Sevens make these associative connections instantly and share them in rapid fire, using voices filled with enthusiasm and energy.

Worldview | The world lacks a bigger plan full of possibilities; I must generate these.

Beliefs | "Life is full of endless possibilities; why worry when you can be happy?"

Motivation | having a life filled with pleasure, constant excitement, and unbounded freedom

Avoidance | pain or discomfort and a life of constraints and limitations

Likes | stimulation - excitement - innovation

Dislikes | not being listened to - negativity - feeling trapped

Growth areas | Sevens are impulsive, unfocused, and rebellious. Even when doing something that they like, they become easily distracted when something else catches their attention. As a result, Sevens typically do one of the following: do not fully complete tasks, finish tasks late, or have to work excessively hard at the last minute to complete their work on time. Because they multi-task to an extreme, they become easily over-extended and exhausted and use humor to defuse serious situations, sometimes inappropriately and ineffectively. When difficulties arise, someone puts constraints on them, or they become bored – which happens often – their minds and bodies move even more quickly than normal. Sevens then become impatient, often reframing the situation as something positive rather than something negative. However, through targeted development work on these specific growth areas, Sevens can achieve their deepest longing.

Deepest longing | feeling complete, whole, and solid

The Rock

EIGHTS pursue the truth, like to keep situations under control, want to make important things happen, and try to hide their vulnerability.

Rocks (EIGHTS) search for control and justice and avoid feeling vulnerable or weak. Symbolized by the mountain made of super-strong rock, Eights are solid and often immovable, strong, and difficult to penetrate.

Assertive, bold, and confident, Eights are highly independent, with a tendency to both protect and control people and events around them and a deep commitment to truth, justice, and equity or fairness. Most Eights are excessive in some way, particularly when they feel anxious or vulnerable. Because they strongly prefer to not show this side of themselves to others, perceiving such feelings as signaling weakness, Eights mask their tender side by engaging in excessiveness in a variety of forms: over-work, too much or too little exercise; erratic, excessive or unhealthy eating; and other forms of over-consumption, such as constant shopping or the acquiring of items — sometimes expensive ones — that they don't really need.

Eights want to get their needs met and go after what they want, try to make big things happen quickly, much akin to moving mountains, and most have a big presence even when they are saying little. Eights also can appear somewhat different from one another. Some Eights are quiet with a low threshold for frustration and an ability to survive and gain control in almost any situation; other Eights are social rebels and protective of others to an extreme; and some Eights are highly emotional, extraordinarily passionate, and enjoy being more center stage.

The Eight's interpersonal style is assertive, and they use voice modulation and non-verbal behavior for effect and impact. For example, they may use a strident voice, direct eye contact, and move closer to others as a way to take charge or make their point, or they may use a softer voice tone, warm eye contact, and a smile to appear gracious, hospitable, or non-threatening.

Worldview | The powerful try to take advantage of the weak; I must change this.

Beliefs | "I must take charge or everything will fall apart; I can handle anything."

Motivation | being in control, establishing justice, and taking immediate, big action

Avoidance | feeling vulnerable, weak, or dependent

Likes | power and influence - honesty - control

Dislikes | people who act like victims - being blind-sided, especially by someone they trust - people who don't take responsibility for their own behavior

Growth areas | Eights are controlling and demanding, with such high expectations for themselves and others that even they have trouble meeting these expectations. While they protect the weak, they also dislike weakness in others and hide their own weakness and vulnerability, even from themselves. Eights work excessively, often to the point of sheer exhaustion, and think that if they relax their efforts, everything will fall apart. They don't trust easily, and when they have a negative reaction to someone, it is almost impossible to get them to change their minds. Eights become angry easily and when they feel wronged, they take action to rebalance the score. However, through targeted development work on these specific growth areas, Eights can achieve their deepest longing.

Deepest longing | regaining their lost innocence while still feeling strong and vital

The 9 Enneagram Types | Enneagram Nines

The Harmonizer

NINES seek peace, harmony, and positive mutual regard, and dislike conflict, tension, and ill will.

Harmonizers (NINES) search for harmony and comfort and avoid tension and conflict. Symbolized by yin and yang, Nines try to reconcile oppositional ideas, forces, and perspectives as a way to have all perspectives considered.

Relaxed, easy to relate to, and accepting, Nines perceive and honor multiple viewpoints and are usually excellent facilitators, drawing out the ideas of others so everyone gets heard. While they value harmony, seek comfortable ways of relating, and are often adept mediators of conflict between and among others, most Nines are extremely uncomfortable with conflict when it's directed toward them and even more uncomfortable when they feel angry with someone else. As a result, Nines keep themselves from doing anything that might generate conflict or create disharmony; they keep themselves from being aware that they are upset; don't express opinions or preferences that could cause discord or disagreements; and diffuse their attention by engaging in activities that comfort them, rather than focus them on their own desires or priorities. As examples, Nines may do some of the following: watch television for hours, flipping television channels on a regular basis; cut the grass or work in the garden when they have projects at work or home they should be doing; go shopping or walk the dog for extended periods of time as a way of avoiding what they should be doing; or even do the dishes in an overly thorough way rather than have a difficult conversation with someone or do work they don't feel like doing.

While Nines appear easygoing on the outside, many experience some degree of internal tension, and they are not always as non-judgmental as they appear. In addition, some Nines tend to satisfy their desire for comfort through the satisfaction of their physical needs — for example, eating, sleeping, and/or reading; some Nines submerge themselves in service of group needs by working extraordinary hours, which allows them to forget about their own desires; and other Nines find such comfort in fusing or blending almost completely with other people who are important to them that they lose a sense of themselves in the process.

The Nine's interpersonal style is agreeable, relatively unassertive, and non-invasive, and they are often able to talk with others about a variety of topics in an easy-going manner. For example, Nines often nod their heads in affirmation or say "Uh, huh," which doesn't mean they agree with the other person, just that they heard what was said. Affable and humorous, they express themselves indirectly rather than boldly or directly as a way to create and maintain positive relationships and reduce potential discord between themselves and others.

Worldview | Everyone deserves to be respected and heard: I must enable this.

Beliefs | "If we could all just get along, life would be peaceful; it's essential to listen to everyone and hear all perspectives."

Motivation | living a peaceful, comfortable, and harmonious life

Avoidance | anger, conflict, ill will, or tension

Likes | respectful behavior - relaxation - comfort

Dislikes | people who don't listen or who are rude - chronic complainers - pushy people

Growth areas | Nines avoid conflict, particularly when they are directly involved, and this causes them to not say what they really think and feel. When someone tries to control a Nine or they feel pressured in any way, Nines may act as if they agree to comply with the request, but then delay doing it or don't do it at all. Nines neglect themselves, their deepest desires, and even their daily preferences as a way to keep the peace with others, but at a price to themselves. When they feel overworked, pressured, or stressed, they procrastinate by doing non-essential activities and, as a result, don't meet deadlines or commitments. However, through targeted development work on these specific growth areas, Nines can achieve their deepest longing.

Deepest longing | knowing that they matter enough to both speak the truth and take values-based action

3 Centers of Intelligence

The 9 Enneagram types are rooted in the Eastern concept of the 3 Centers of Intelligence: the Head or Mental Center, the Heart or Emotional Center, and the Body or Instinctual Center, also referred to as the Physical Center. The 3 Centers of Intelligence have great importance in the Enneagram.

First, all of us have all 3 Centers of Intelligence, but we don't always use them well. The real goal or purpose of using the Enneagram isn't really about knowing our type number and using this information as a guide for growth through understanding our type-based patterns of thinking, feeling and behaving. It is about personal and spiritual integration through accessing and utilizing each of our 3 Centers of Intelligence in their most productive ways.

To that end, once we know our Enneagram type, we gain precise insight into how we both use and misuse each Center of Intelligence based on our type. Even more, there are specific development activities based on our type that enable greater access to each Center.

Finally, the 9 Enneagram types are actually organized according to the 3 Centers of Intelligence with three Enneagram types being formed in each of the 3 Centers of Intelligence. Specifically, the three Head Center types (Five, Six and Seven) are from the Mental Center and are three different responses to the central emotion of that center: fear. The three Heart Center types (Two, Three and Four) are formed from the Heart Center, representing three different ways of creating an image that others will, hopefully, respond to affirmatively. The central emotion associated with the Heart Center is sorrow, a sadness that comes from being affirmed for one's image but not one's truer self. The three Body Center types (Eight, Nine and One) are created from the Body or Instinctual Center and represent three different responses to the emotion of anger. In addition, the Body Center types also share the theme of being in control and a tendency to take action or go to inaction.

Throughout this book, the type-based responses of clients at different stages of the consulting process are grouped according to Centers of Intelligence, and the reason for this is that there are strong similarities and also differences in how individuals formed from the same Center of Intelligence respond. More detail on the three types formed in each Center of Intelligence is provided on the following pages.

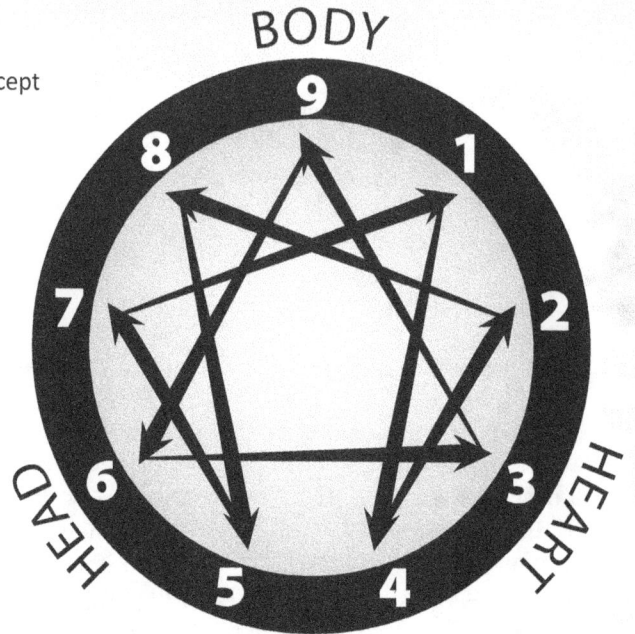

Head Center Functions

Gather information | Generate ideas | Engage in mental processing | Rational analysis | Planning

Productive Uses
Objective analysis | Astute insight | Productive planning

Misuses
Overanalyzing | Projection | Overplanning

Enneagram Style	Three Ways of Responding to Fear	Most Common Misuse of Head Center
Five	Withdraw and depend solely on their own resources; gather abundant information to analyze for the purpose of developing preventive strategies	Overanalyzing
Six	Create continuous anticipatory scenarios in order to overcome potential problems and/or go headlong into fearful situations to prove their own courage	Projection
Seven	Move away from fear by imagining positive future possibilities and by generating exciting ideas rather than feel uncomfortable or anxious	Overplanning

Heart Center Functions

Experience feelings | Relate to others emotionally | Sensitivity to the feelings and reactions of others

Productive Uses
Empathy | Authentic relating | Compassion

Misuses
Emotional manipulation | Playing roles | Oversensitivity

Enneagram Style	Three Ways of Creating an Image	Most Common Misuse of Heart Center
Two	Create an image of being likable, generous, and concerned for other people, then look to others for affirmation of their self-worth	Emotional manipulation
Three	Project an image of self-confidence and success, then seek the respect and admiration of others for what they accomplish	Playing roles
Four	Create an image of being unique, special, and different, then use their emotional sensitivity to avoid feeling not good enough	Oversensitivity

Body Center Functions

Movement | Experience physical sensations | Take action or inaction | Control of one's environment

Productive Uses
Taking effective action | Steadfastness | Gut knowing

Misuses
Excessive action | Passivity | Reactivity

Enneagram Style	Three Ways of Responding to Anger	Most Common Misuse of Body Center
Eight	Readily express anger, starting from the gut, and believe that anger is simply energy that needs release	Excessive action
Nine	Avoid anger – both their own and that of others – and seek instead to mediate differences and create harmony	Passivity
One	Manifest anger as resentment, irritation, or continual small eruptions; believe anger is a negative emotion that must be kept under control	Reactivity

CHAPTER 2
FOUNDATIONS | CONSULTING with THE ENNEAGRAM

If you have built castles in the air, your work need not be lost;
that is where they should be. Now put the foundations under them.
Henry David Thoreau

Successful organizational change efforts of all kinds –
leadership, teams, communication, redesigns, strategy, and
conflict, just as examples – require the consultant to have a
strong foundation in the field of organization development
(OD). The following items will help you develop the foundation
you need to become an excellent consultant using the
Enneagram in your consulting work:

Linkages between OD and the Enneagram

Organization development map

Consulting with the Enneagram
core competency assessment

6-C consulting model

Action research overview

Consultant roles

Systems model

Experiential learning cycle

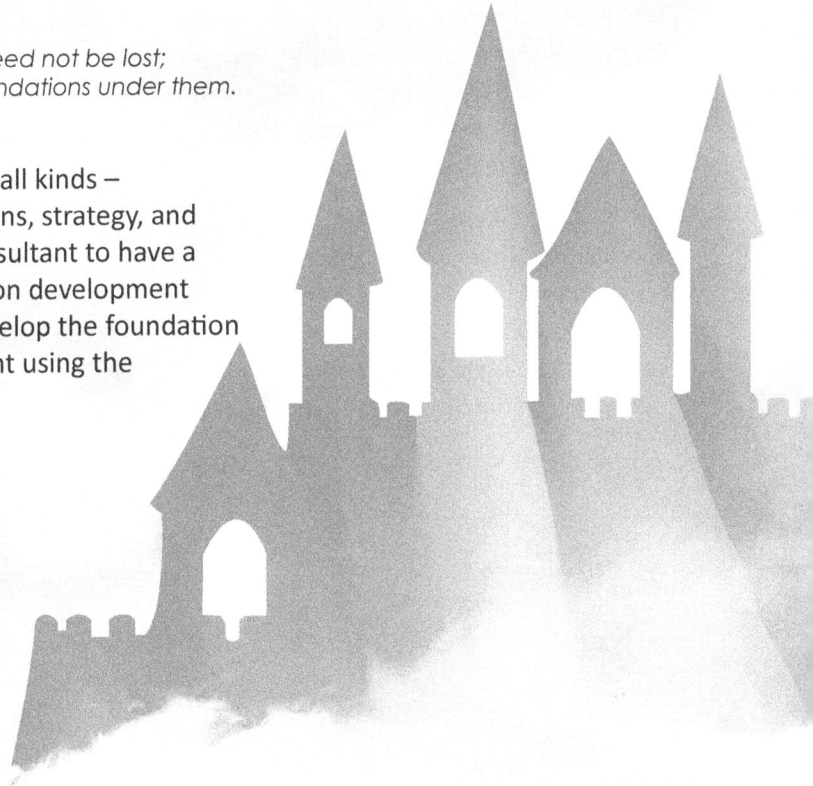

Organization Development and the Enneagram

The field known as organization development (OD) and the pathway known as the Enneagram are quite different, yet remarkably similar. OD is relatively young (60+ years old), while the Enneagram is ancient (4000+ years). We know where OD started (in the late 1940s through the work on National Training Labs), but we are less clear about the Enneagram's exact origins. OD looks at change strategies for organizations, teams, pairs, and individuals, while the Enneagram focuses on individual consciousness and development.

But their similarities are also striking. The intent of both systems (OD and the Enneagram) is transformation, although both systems can be used for incremental improvement. Both systems believe that people and systems can change and provide an architecture and technology for doing so. Both OD and the Enneagram take a holistic, systems approach to understanding the way things work as well as the way things change. Even more similarities can be seen in the chart on the following page.

	Organization Development	**The Enneagram**
What is it?	"OD is an organizational improvement strategy that uses behavioral science principles and practices to improve individual and organizational effectiveness." ~ French, Bell & Zawacki, 2000	The Enneagram is an ancient characterological system that uses psychological, spiritual, and other human development principles and practices to enhance human consciousness at the individual and group level.
Core Technologies	"The key aspects of the model are diagnosis, data gathering, feedback to the client group, data discussion and work by the client group, action planning, and action. The sequence tends to be cyclical, with the focus on new or advanced problems as the client group learns to work more effectively together." ~ French & Bell, 1999	The most commonly used methodologies used to learn the Enneagram include the following: data collection through self-observation, guided sharing of one's own personal stories, group dialogue, panels, and individual, pair, and small to large group activities.
Core Values*	Quality of life – satisfaction with whole life experience Health, human potentiality, empowerment, growth, and excellence Freedom and responsibility Justice – fairness and rightness for everyone Dignity, integrity, worth and fundamental rights of all levels of human systems All-win attitudes and cooperation Authenticity and openness in relationships Effectiveness, efficiency, and alignment Holistic, system view, and stakeholder orientation Wide participation in system affairs	Life and work satisfaction Health, human potentiality, empowerment, growth, and excellence Freedom and responsibility Full acceptance of self and others Dignity, integrity, and self-worth Authenticity and openness in relationships Effectiveness, alignment, and integration Holistic, systemic view of self and others Choice in all aspects of life
Ethical Standards*	Interventions must be selected that have a high probability of being helpful in the particular situation The consultant should not use interventions that exceed her or his expertise The client system should be as informed as is practical about the nature of the process The consultant must not be working any personal, hidden agendas that obtrude into high-quality service for the client Commitments to confidentiality must be kept The client must not be promised unrealistic outcomes	Activities must be selected that have a high probability of being helpful in the particular situation The "teacher" engages only in working within his or her area of expertise Client(s) are informed about the nature of the process and outcomes The "teacher" must not be working any personal, hidden agendas, or manipulate the client(s) Commitments to confidentiality must be kept The client(s) must not be promised unrealistic outcomes

* Organization development items are taken from *International Organization Development Code of Ethics Guidelines*

OD provides a coherent set of theories and practices to enable change in human systems, but it does so at the generic human level. The Enneagram provides a comprehensive architecture with theory and practice that enables change in individuals. Put together, they provide a powerhouse of change and transformation.

Organization Development Consulting Map

ACTION RESEARCH

SYSTEMS CHANGE THEORY

PRINCIPLES AND VALUES

CONSULTING SKILLS

SUB-THEORIES

Stages	Contracting	Collecting	Communicating
Consulting Tasks	Clarify problem | issues Agree on project goals | outcomes Create a project overview Develop initial contract	Design data collection process Collect data Analyze data	Prepare report | presentation Plan feedback meeting Produce feedback materials Conduct feedback meeting Do collaborative diagnosis
Consulting Skills	Rapport building Issue identification Knowledge of relevant OD frameworks and processes Diagnosis Project management	**Data Collection** Data collection methodologies Constructing questions Interviewing Focus groups Survey development **Data Analysis** Data analysis techniques Quantitative data Qualitative data Relevant conceptual frameworks Theme identification Systems thinking Diagnosis	Meeting planning Material design Giving and receiving feedback Coaching Facilitation
Consultant's Use of Self	Self-mastery Confidence Active listening	Mental | emotional | physical integration Ability to access rational and intuitive information	Empathy Respect Compassion

Adapted from the work of NTL.

ACTION RESEARCH

SYSTEMS CHANGE THEORY

PRINCIPLES AND VALUES

CONSULTING SKILLS

SUB-THEORIES

Stages	Challenging	Changing	Closing
Consulting Tasks	Identify areas where action is needed Challenge client to take action	Assess critical change areas Prioritize action areas Develop action plan Clarify interventions and preferred technology Conduct intervention	Review goals and outcomes Assess progress Identify any new issues Bring closure End Phase out Re-contract
Consulting Skills	Understanding client's needs Confrontation Support	Intervention technologies Practices related to change technologies Meeting design skills Facilitation Project management Visual capabilities Chart pads PowerPoint	Evaluation technology Issue identification Diagnosis Re-contracting skills Closure skills
Consultant's Use of Self	Courage Support Challenge	Authenticity Non-reactivity Objectivity	Express feelings Receive feedback Model closure

Consulting Competency Model

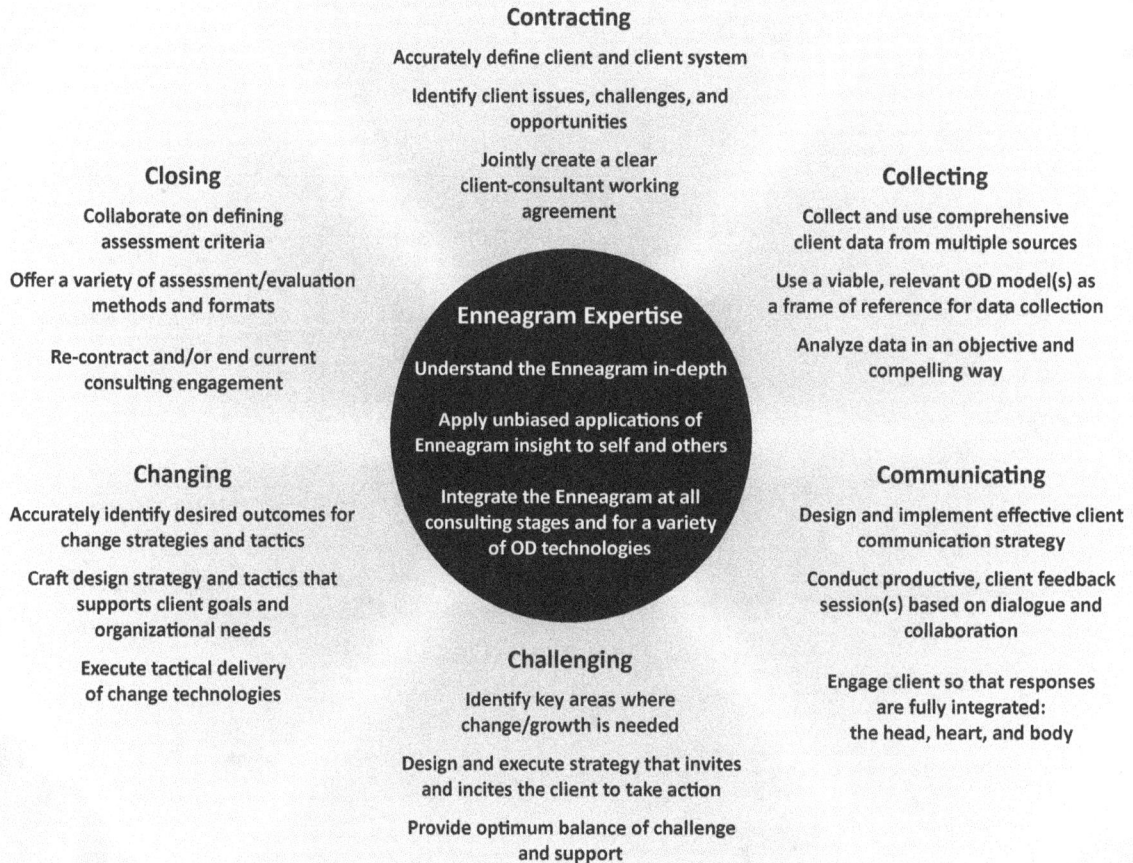

Contracting

Accurately define client and client system

Identify client issues, challenges, and opportunities

Jointly create a clear client-consultant working agreement

Closing

Collaborate on defining assessment criteria

Offer a variety of assessment/evaluation methods and formats

Re-contract and/or end current consulting engagement

Collecting

Collect and use comprehensive client data from multiple sources

Use a viable, relevant OD model(s) as a frame of reference for data collection

Analyze data in an objective and compelling way

Enneagram Expertise

Understand the Enneagram in-depth

Apply unbiased applications of Enneagram insight to self and others

Integrate the Enneagram at all consulting stages and for a variety of OD technologies

Changing

Accurately identify desired outcomes for change strategies and tactics

Craft design strategy and tactics that supports client goals and organizational needs

Execute tactical delivery of change technologies

Communicating

Design and implement effective client communication strategy

Conduct productive, client feedback session(s) based on dialogue and collaboration

Engage client so that responses are fully integrated: the head, heart, and body

Challenging

Identify key areas where change/growth is needed

Design and execute strategy that invites and incites the client to take action

Provide optimum balance of challenge and support

Consulting with the Enneagram Core Competency Assessment

This consultant competency self-assessment is intended as a tool to help you assess your current level of competencies as a consultant who uses the Enneagram in organizations. The self-assessment can then be used to focus your further growth.

Instructions | With a mindset of exploring your *self*, please respond to each item by placing an "**X**" in the box that best reflects your perception of your own skills.

Reflection Questions | At the end of the assessment, there are three *Reflection Questions* for you to complete, based on your review of your overall responses.

	low	ok	good	great
Enneagram Expertise				
I have an in-depth understanding of Enneagram systems and styles.	☐	☐	☐	☐
I can apply Enneagram insights in an unbiased way.	☐	☐	☐	☐
I have in-depth skills in a wide variety of Enneagram-business applications.	☐	☐	☐	☐
Contracting (and entry)				
I can accurately clarify who the client is for the project.	☐	☐	☐	☐
I can collaborate with clients to identify key issues, challenges, and opportunities.	☐	☐	☐	☐
I can create an effective client-consultant contract (verbal and written).	☐	☐	☐	☐
Collecting				
I know how to collect comprehensive client data from multiple sources.	☐	☐	☐	☐
I have a wide repertoire of behavioral science and OD theories and models.	☐	☐	☐	☐
I can objectively analyze data so that it becomes diagnostic and actionable.	☐	☐	☐	☐
Communicating				
I can design an effective data-feedback communication strategy tailored to the client.	☐	☐	☐	☐
I can facilitate client feedback that enhances communication via dialogue and listening.	☐	☐	☐	☐
I can engage the client at multiple levels of response: head, heart, and body.	☐	☐	☐	☐
Challenging				
I can accurately identify and prioritize the most important areas for the client's growth.	☐	☐	☐	☐
I can develop and execute strategies that challenge the client to take action.	☐	☐	☐	☐
I can find the optimal balance between support and challenge for each client.	☐	☐	☐	☐
Changing				
I can accurately select desired outcomes for change strategies and tactics.	☐	☐	☐	☐
I know existing change technologies or can design new ones, as needed.	☐	☐	☐	☐
I can skillfully implement a wide variety of change tactics, as needed.	☐	☐	☐	☐
Closing				
I can determine success criteria (long and short-term) for change initiatives.	☐	☐	☐	☐
I have in-depth knowledge of assessment methods, plus when to use them.	☐	☐	☐	☐
I know when to re-contract with clients and when to end the consultation.	☐	☐	☐	☐

Reflection Questions

Question 1 | Review your scores for *each question* on the assessment and write down the three areas you believe are your greatest strengths.

Question 2 | Review your scores for *each question* on the assessment and write down the three areas you believe are your greatest development areas.

Question 3 | What will you do to utilize your strengths and work on your development needs?

6-C Consulting Model

Head Center
1. **C**ontracting, including entry
2. **C**ollecting data and data analysis

Heart Center
3. **C**ommunicating the data
4. **C**hallenging action

Body Center
5. **C**hanging the organization
6. **C**losing the consultation

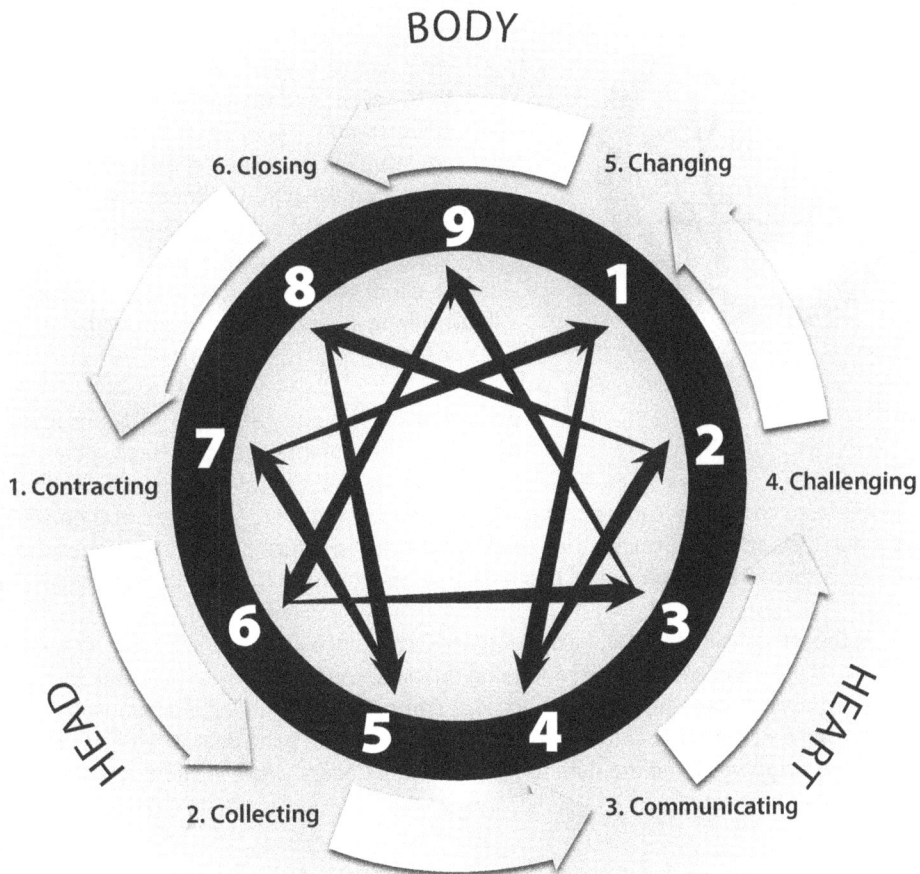

BODY

6. Closing

5. Changing

1. Contracting

4. Challenging

HEAD

HEART

2. Collecting

3. Communicating

6-C Consulting Model

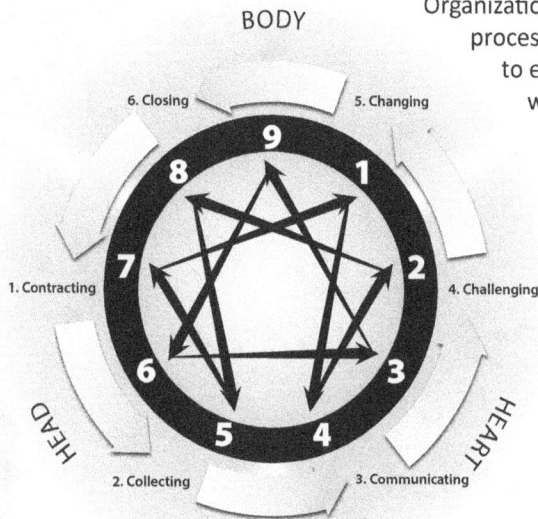

Organization development (OD) consulting involves a step-by-step process that begins with *Contracting*, conversing with the client to establish a working agreement for how the consultation will proceed; *Collecting* real and unbiased data in order to discover problem areas as well as future possibilities, then analyzing the information gathered in a coherent and diagnostic way; *Communicating* the analyzed data to the client and the client system so they can fully understand the root causes and underlying factors involved in the desired change; *Challenging* the client to take action so there is sufficient energy and urgency to take action; *Changing* the organization in a systematic and sustainable way; and, finally, *Closing* the client engagement, which may mean ending the consulting altogether or re-contracting for additional work as needed.

From an Enneagram perspective, an OD consultant needs to have all three Centers of Intelligence – Head, Heart, and Body – available to him or her at all times during the consultation. Only a fully embodied and integrated consultant can help clients and client organizations access all of themselves to bring to the change, whether it is a specific problem that needs addressing, a future possibility or innovation that needs to be implemented, a change in culture that is being desired, or a team that needs to work better together.

In addition, during the 6-C consulting cycle, each Center of Intelligence plays a special role. In the first two stages, *Contracting* with the client and *Collecting* and analyzing the data, the Head Center plays the lead role, with the other two Centers of Intelligence in supporting functions; *Contracting* and *Collecting* involve the planning, data gathering and analyzing functions that come from the Head Center. Once the data is ready for the client, and the consultation moves to *Communicating* the data to the client and *Challenging* the client to take action, the Heart Center becomes more prominent.

During these stages, the task is to craft the best strategy for effectively communicating with the client and to develop the optimum level of challenge so that the client feels resourced and empowered; these are functions of the Heart Center – relationships, communication, and empathy. Finally, the last two stages of the 6-C Consulting Model – *Changing* and *Closing* – rely more on the Body Center, the Center of Intelligence that focuses on action and control. During the *Changing* stage, the client needs to take "right action" and to do so in both a comprehensive and detailed way. In the *Closing* stage, action is still the subtext: should the project end, or be continued because there is more needed for completion, or should there be a re-contract for entirely new consulting work.

Of course, consulting always contains unpredictable events and new opportunities – for example, the client receives a promotion or gets fired, a new problem arises that provides a change of direction but also a consulting opportunity, or an organizational change alters the consulting requirements. Because of these factors, effective consulting must be partly emergent, flexible, and spontaneous.

At the same time, however, consultations must also be predictable; the 6-C Consulting Model provides this predictability. Following this model – and following it in sequence – ensures predictability and dramatically increases the chances of a successful outcome, since the model provides for a clear plan rather than an open-ended process that may or may not lead to the intended results.

The consulting process must also hold the consultant and the client accountable for the results. Accountability is built into the consulting model here, with both the consultant and the client sharing the responsibility for honoring the negotiated consulting agreements.

While the consulting process begins with Stage 1, *Contracting*, and ends with Stage 6, *Closing*, the consulting process is not always linear; often it is circular. For example, upon completing the 6-C consulting cycle, the consultant and client may agree to re-contract and begin the whole cycle anew. Similarly, during Stages 2, 3, 4, or even 5, the consultant and client may decide to shift their direction; when this occurs, they need to re-contract and begin a new 6-C consulting cycle.

Action Research Overview

OD interventions (data-based designed actions) are conducted only after the initial stages of an organization development engagement have been completed – that is, after contracting, collecting data, communicating the data, and challenging the client to take action.

Action Research forms the basis for all organization interventions because it is data based, relying on real data from the client system and larger organization to determine the most effective change strategies. In Action Research, the principle is that not only do you use data as the basis for determining the best course of action, but you also learn as you go based on the action taken. This means that as you move forward, you may need to shift direction based on new information.

The chart on the following page lists the stages of an OD consultation as well as the most important questions for the OD consultant. Although the stages appear linear, the process is actually a cycle in which re-contracting, assessing and redesigning are done on an as-needed basis.

Consulting Stage	Tasks	Key Questions for Consultant
Contracting Entry and contracting	Create initial contact Define issues, needs, challenges, and opportunities Distinguish between client's "presenting" need and possible "real need" Explore client's readiness for change Agree on consulting contract	Who is "real client"? Are there others other than the "real client" who need to be involved and how? Who is the "client system"? Do I want (and do I have) the skills to do this work? Do I want to work with this client? What agreements need to be made to create an effective, workable client-consultant contract?
Collecting Data collection, analysis, and diagnosis	Conduct a comprehensive data collection Analyze data, using a diagnostic approach that highlights key issues and themes as well as root causes	What are most appropriate OD models to use for this data collection? What types of data are needed to understand the key issues, organizational factors, and the environmental context to lead to the root causes? Who collects the data and how should it be collected?
Communicating Data feedback	Prepare diagnostic data summary Feedback findings and diagnosis to client	What is the most effective way to structure the diagnostic feedback session? How can I help the client understand the findings, the diagnosis and how they relate to the selection of potential interventions? How do I collaborate with the client during the diagnosis phase? How do the client and I develop a shared understanding of the key issues? How do these issues related to one another?
Challenging	Identify critical issues to be addressed Gain client commitment to action	What will encourage the client to make effective choices and to take productive and timely action? How do I balance the level of support and challenge for this particular client?
Changing Action planning and implementation	Develop action plan, including a strategy for implementation Implement action plan	How do I involve the client in the design of the intervention? What are the desired outcomes of the intervention? How do I ensure that the intervention has an appropriate balance of risk-taking and stability? How do we build in feedback and adjustments to the action taken? How can we build in early and visible successes? How do we adjust the timing of the intervention to align with ongoing work of the client?
Closing Assessment, institutionalization of the change, and separation	Compare outcomes of the intervention to initial goals and assess the quality of results Client "adopts" the change Consultant disengagement or re-contracting	What assessment methods can be used to indicate what changes actually occurred and what can be done to enhance the results? How can I help the client system develop ongoing internal leadership, knowledge, and skills to sustain and improve the change on their own? What are the proper conditions for me to return to the client for additional support for this change effort? How can the client and I know when to conclude this consulting contract?

Consultant Roles

Consultants need to be clear about the consulting role they are expected to play, but also which role will be the most beneficial to the success of the client engagement. In addition, the client may have expectations of the consultant based on his or her assumption of the role the consultant should be playing. If the client and consultant have different expectations, these need to be resolved very early. An OD consultant usually plays the process consultant role, but the best role is a combination of strategic business partner and process consultant.

CONSULTANT ROLE	TYPICAL WORK	USEFUL WHEN...	NOT USEFUL WHEN...
Authoritative Expert Based on the doctor-patient model (*I can fix you*), the consultant is perceived as the resident *expert* in terms of the content, strategy, and tasks and is responsible for results.	**Does what clients can't or won't do for themselves** Diagnose problems Generate solutions Predict consequences Make recommendations	Client dealing with unfamiliar problem Client has no expertise and doesn't need to develop it There is a crisis or deadline requiring a quick solution Client's buy-in not crucial	Client needs to have buy-in to solution to make it work Problem definition is unclear Early, fast solutions not needed Client needs to develop expertise and/or change needs to be sustainable
Skilled Tactician The client perceives the consultant as an outsourced vendor such that the consultant is expected to apply specialized knowledge and skills toward goals and tasks defined solely by the client.	**Implements plan and tactics designed by the organization** Client specifies the needed work Consultant develops work-plan or implements existing plan Goal is to make organization more effective, not to develop individuals, teams or to generate creative solutions	Client makes accurate diagnosis of what is needed Client willingly "owns" the outcome of the work Problem or change is unique and non-repetitive Development of organizational personnel has little organizational benefit	Collaboration is required Consultant needs some degree of influence or input into the work Client ultimately needs to develop the knowledge and skills
Strategic Business Partner The consultant and client form a trusting, 50/50 relationship in which the consultant does not solve client's problems, but applies specialized process or content knowledge to help clients solve their own problems.	**Fully understands the client's business and focuses on client's strategy** Helps client recognize, define, diagnose, and solve problems independently Work is a collaborative effort Consultant is on-call as well as working on medium and long-term issues	Client willing to take primary responsibility for outcomes Problems are complex Strong need for organizational commitment to solutions Client needs a trustworthy, honest sounding board Client wants a long-term consulting relationship	Client needs quick solution Client needs specialized expertise Client not interested in a strategic partnership Pending crisis needs immediate resolution
Process Consultant The consultant focuses on individual, interpersonal, team, organizational, and inter-organizational processes in service of increased awareness, choice, effectiveness, growth, and sustainability.	**Focuses on process issues that hinder effectiveness and works with client and client system to make needed changes** Helps clients identify process-related issues and recognize their impact on multiple levels of the organization	Client willing to take primary responsibility for changes and new behaviors Client willingly solicits and uses feedback The problems are process-related and changeable	Client resists feedback and is not open to new learning There is a specific task or product needed as an outcome Client or client system is not empowered to change Client expects consultant to tell them what to do

Organizations | A Systems Model

Models of organizations are actually theories that make an attempt to describe reality. Systems models are better than most because they illuminate only the organization's systems and subsystems, and they also clarify the interrelationships between these elements. In other words, systems models define the most important organizational elements and how they impact one another. This perspective helps with data collection, diagnosis of core issues, and the development of essential change strategies and tactics.

The systems model below is but one example of an organizational systems model, and there are many other excellent ones. This particular model highlights leadership as a fundamental element, defines six other important subsystems, includes specific environmental components, and is also a "thru-put" model. "Thru-put" models show how different factors move through an organization via inputs and outputs. Remember that theories and models are simply approximations of reality.

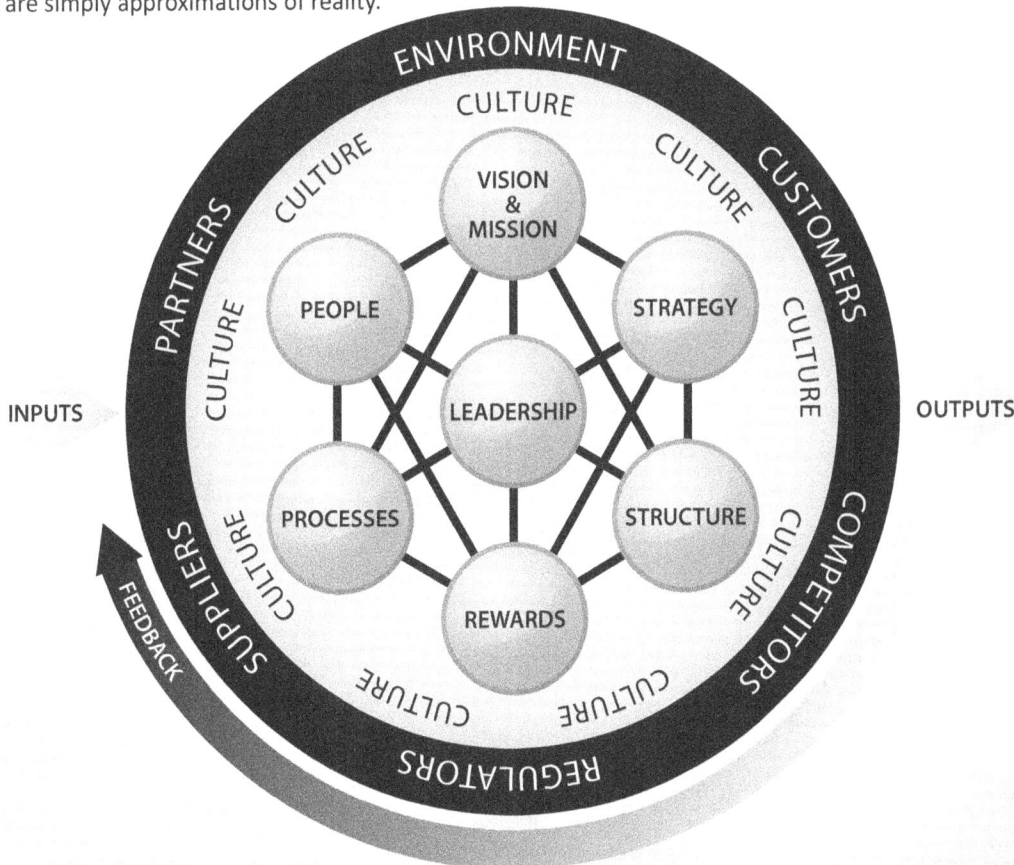

Experiential Learning Cycle

Organization Development and the Action Research Method are both based on the 6-step Experiential Learning Cycle. Throughout every stage of a consultation, both the consultant and client engage in a cycle of "learning from what was done" and "doing based on what was learned."

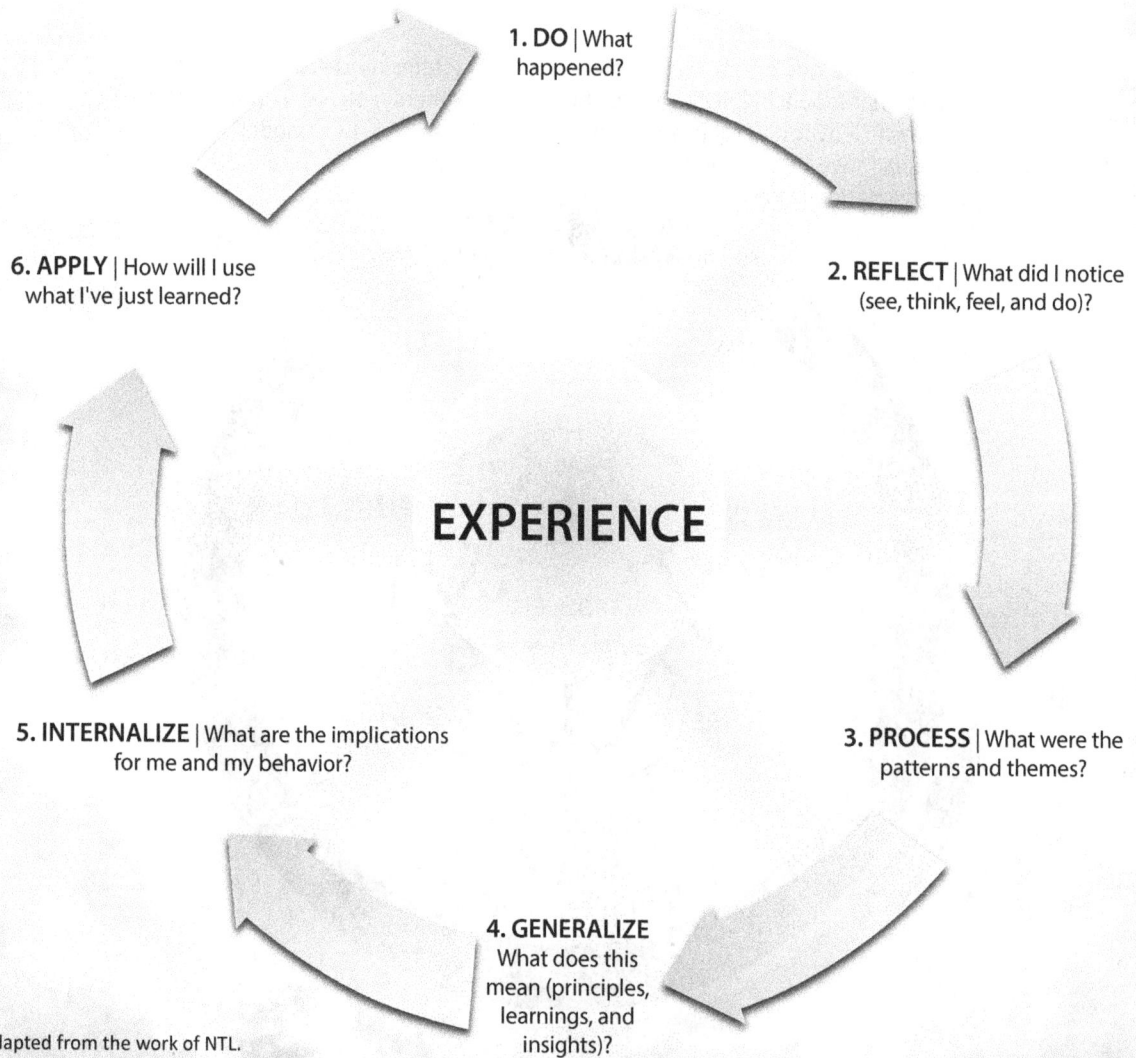

1. DO | What happened?

2. REFLECT | What did I notice (see, think, feel, and do)?

3. PROCESS | What were the patterns and themes?

4. GENERALIZE What does this mean (principles, learnings, and insights)?

5. INTERNALIZE | What are the implications for me and my behavior?

6. APPLY | How will I use what I've just learned?

EXPERIENCE

Adapted from the work of NTL.

CHAPTER 3
CONTRACTING | CONSULTING with THE ENNEAGRAM

Only free men can negotiate; prisoners cannot enter into contracts.
Your freedom and mine cannot be separated.
Nelson Mandela

Effective contracting is the most important part of the consulting process because it sets agreements and expectations, preventing misunderstandings later on. Contracting involves far more than defining project outcomes, deliverables, timetables and pricing. Covering both the project-related tasks and the consulting relationships is a fine-tuned dance that the consultant needs to lead in a collaborative fashion. In addition, the contract gives both you and the client a reference point to discuss the project's progress, make mid-course changes and adjustments, and even re-contract as necessary. Most experienced consultants say that when they have had projects in which difficulties arouse, the issues almost always were related to the initial contracting stage. The following information will help you deal with all the intricacies of contracting.

Starting the work | the consultant-client match

Contracting and the Enneagram

Contracting competency assessment

Post-contracting checklist

Elements of a consulting proposal

Sample proposals

To begin the consulting process, you need to have a client and a consultant. Hopefully, both are good! In addition to the consultant possessing skills and experience in the area the client wants work, the match or fit between the client and consultant is extremely important. Here's what to look for:

What to look for in a consultant

Prior success as a consultant

Availability

Credibility

Good judgment

Organizational savvy

Excellent listening skills

Establishes rapport easily

Someone you respect

What to look for in a client

Has the required authority to make the needed changes

Honesty

Willingness to learn

A moderate to high degree of self-awareness

Commitment to the consulting process

Someone you don't dislike

You may have noticed that *liking* the consultant is not included on the list of what to look for in a consultant. While liking the consultant can be beneficial, it is far more important that the client *respect* the consultant. On the "what to look for in a client" list, the phrasing "someone you don't dislike" has been purposefully chosen rather than "someone you like": the consultant does not have to really like the client, only to have no aversive reaction to him or her. If the consultant were to dislike the client, that individual would most likely sense the consultant's negativity, even if the consultant tried to hide it. When a client respects the consultant and the consultant doesn't dislike the client, *and* the consulting achieves tangible results, in nearly every case the consultant and client develop a mutual liking and appreciation over the course of the consulting.

Contracting and the Enneagram

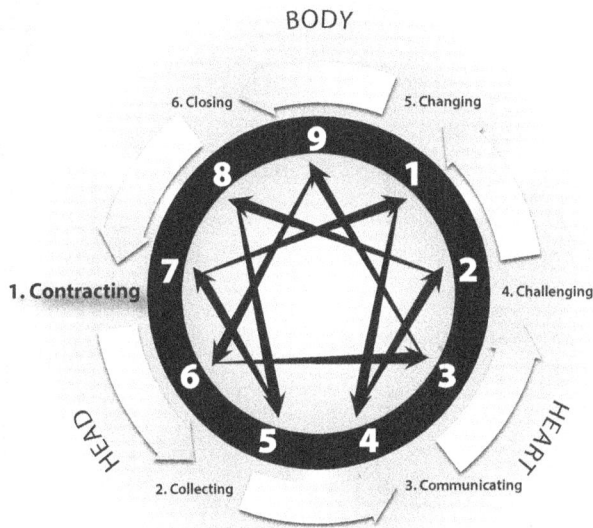

BODY

6. Closing   5. Changing

9
8   1
1. **Contracting**   7   2   4. Challenging
6   3
5   4

HEAD

HEART

2. Collecting   3. Communicating

6-C Consulting Model

CONTRACTING FOCUS AREAS

What are the consultation goals, outcomes, and deliverables?

Who is the "real client" and who else needs to be involved (and in what roles)?

What consulting methodology (processes) will be used for various project components, including assessing results?

What is the overall strategy and plan, including logistics and timetables?

How will the client-consultant relationship work? What is confidential?

To become not just a good consultant but a great one requires an understanding of both the science and the art of consulting. The science of consulting can be learned from the 6-C Consulting Model. The art of consulting can be enhanced through use of the insights of the Enneagram as this knowledge allows the consultant to tailor the consulting process to the Enneagram style of the client.

Contracting – and entry into the client's world and system – is the most important stage of every consulting engagement. *Contracting* involves discussions and interactions between the consultant and the client that can range from one meeting to many weeks or even months. During these conversations (whether by phone, email, or in-person), the client and consultant get to know each other better in their new roles, discuss their expectations and, ultimately, reach a collaborative and mutually agreed-upon consulting plan. This plan includes concurrence on the following areas:

Establishing the goals (outcomes/intentions/deliverables) for the consultation

Clarifying who else (in addition to the main client) needs to be involved and in what role – for example, the immediate boss or human resource personnel

Confirming the consulting methodology, including what approaches will be used, what data will be collected, how the data will be gathered, and from whom

Defining the logistics and timetables of the consulting, such as duration, frequency, and schedule of the consulting sessions, as well as the general structure of the consulting process

Discussing how the relationship will work, covering topics such as preferred working styles and other areas of concern

Developing confidentiality agreements (for both the consultant-client conversations and the project work itself)

What transpires during the *Contracting* stage can make or break the success of the consulting effort. Specifically, effective contracting can prevent many problems that often occur later in a consulting relationship. In addition, ineffective contracting actually creates its own problems, such as confusion, lack of trust, and more. The dual goals of contracting are to address both the basic contracting questions listed above and to raise issues related to the emotional subtext of the consulting conversation. These subtext issues typically involve feelings of trust, perceived value of both the consultant and the consulting, and the need for control. It is far more difficult to discuss these emotional issues than it is to discuss the basic contracting questions, because these emotional concerns are often unconscious and also involve much greater risk. Nonetheless, they are very real and can have a profound impact on the consulting process.

In addressing these implicit issues, a clear yet subtle approach is usually best as it accomplishes the goal without being too threatening. For example, "What other issues related to confidentiality would be helpful to discuss?" is an effective substitute for, "Do you trust me?" Similarly, asking, "What experiences from my background would be useful for me to share with you?" works far better than, "Do you think I have the competence to be your consultant?" Finally, "How do you think we should handle future changes we might want to make in the consulting goals or the consulting relationship?" will elicit a more informative response than would the question, "Do you feel you are going to have enough control in our consulting relationship?"

Enneagram Insights

HEAD CENTER-BASED ISSUE | TRUST

Trust between the consultant and client is crucial to the success of the consulting experience and trust-related issues need to be discussed at the time of contracting. The client must trust that the consultant:

Will maintain confidentiality

Possesses impeccable integrity, and is not having unauthorized side conversations related to the consulting

Will be reliable in the consulting relationship, meaning that he or she will be available to the client when needed

If the client's company has requested the consulting, the client must also have trust in the organization – for example, that there is no ulterior motive behind the consulting, such as an impending demotion, or that anyone in the organization will pressure the consultant to reveal information or to alter the consulting contract. While these issues will be of concern to anyone who agrees to use a consultant, they will be more worrisome for individuals with head-based Enneagram styles (Five, Six, and Seven), as trust and doubt are central to their personalities.

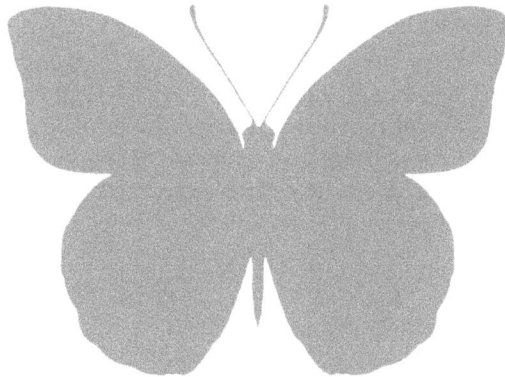

HEART CENTER-BASED ISSUE | VALUE OF THE CONSULTANT AND THE CONSULTING

Value refers to the perceived advantages and benefits to the client that are possible outgrowths of the consulting relationship. During the contracting discussion, clients silently consider whether or not there are sufficient benefits to justify the time and cost of consulting. Factors in the value equation include the level of respect and credibility the consultant commands in the organization, the perceived competence and credibility of the consultant with regard to achieving the consulting goals, and the degree of perceived positive regard that the consultant has for the client. Positive regard is important because it creates an environment in which the client is more likely to feel comfortable about being open; when the client perceives a lack of positive regard from the consultant, the consulting sessions typically have an underlying tension that makes both parties uncomfortable. In addition, the client is usually seeking a consultant who will be forthcoming about information, contacts, and developmental opportunities both within and outside the organization. A consultant who does not have a positive reaction to the client is less likely to be forthcoming. While everyone using a consultant will have the above issues on their minds, the heart-based styles (Two, Three, and Four) will tend to be most concerned about them because of their preoccupation with image and interpersonal acceptance.

BODY CENTER-BASED ISSUE | CONTROL

Issues of *control* usually first appear during the Contracting stage and continue throughout the consulting relationship. Such control issues include who sets the agenda and time for the consulting conversations, who prevails in the event of a difference of opinion or a disagreement about the direction of the consulting, and whether the consultant and the client are well matched (although not necessarily equal) in personal and organizational power. Although individuals of all styles carry these implicit concerns, they tend to be forefront in the minds of the three body-based styles (One, Eight, and Nine) for whom issues of control are central to the personality structure.

Contracting Competency Assessment

This self-assessment is designed to help you identify your strengths and development areas as a consultant, with a focus on the Contracting stage of the consulting project. Check the box next to each question that most reflects your perception of your own skills. Your answers will tell you where you need to focus your future skill development.

	low	ok	good	great
Pre-Contracting | Entry				
Engage in research to learn about the client, organization, and industry.	☐	☐	☐	☐
Think through in advance how to best structure the contracting meeting.	☐	☐	☐	☐
Honestly consider if you have the skills and experience to do this work.	☐	☐	☐	☐
Contracting | Rapport Building				
Engage the client with genuine curiosity, interest, and respect.	☐	☐	☐	☐
Model open communication and dialogue, appropriate to the situation.	☐	☐	☐	☐
Open and responsive to client and client feedback.	☐	☐	☐	☐
Contracting | Issue Identification				
Actively listen to client's definition of needs, issues, and concerns.	☐	☐	☐	☐
Solicit examples re: issues from client, as well as contributing factors.	☐	☐	☐	☐
Demonstrate systems perspective of root causes and system impacts.	☐	☐	☐	☐
Contracting | Goal Setting				
Formulates clear, viable project goals (outcomes) and measurements.	☐	☐	☐	☐
Delineate and confirm all resources required for project success.	☐	☐	☐	☐
Provide clarity re: project roles, scope, strategy, steps, and deliverables.	☐	☐	☐	☐
Contracting | Process				
Manage pace and direction of meeting without being controlling.	☐	☐	☐	☐
Track both the content and the process of what is discussed.	☐	☐	☐	☐
Notice what is not being discussed; raise issues in a non-threatening way.	☐	☐	☐	☐
Contracting | Clarity and Closure				
Manage own feeling responses and behavior in service of the client.	☐	☐	☐	☐
Raise and discuss ethical issues, if relevant to the project.	☐	☐	☐	☐
Conclude meeting clarity about accountabilities and steps moving forward.	☐	☐	☐	☐

Post-Contracting Checklist

It is so important to do a post-consulting phase review to make sure that everything that needed doing was accomplished well and/or to identify areas that still need attention before moving forward in the consultation.

For each contracting topic below, rate yourself (3) well done; (2) needs more work; or (1) didn't do much and needs lots of attention. For items given a 1 or 2 rating, write down what you need to do prior to or during the next client meeting.

CONTRACTING TOPIC	RATING	NEED TO DO
Clear goals (outcomes) and deliverables		
Roles are clear (client(s), consultant(s), others)		
Strong client-consultant relationship built (clarity, trust, openness, authenticity, shared values)		
Required resources available (time, people, money, access)		
Effective consulting plan for moving forward (including structure and processes)		
Data collection basic plan (what, who, how, when)		
Communication strategy and plan (what, who, how, when)		
Necessary level of participation and involvement (what, who, how, when)		
Clear accountabilities		
Measurement and evaluation discussed		

Elements of a Consulting Proposal or Contract

A proposal usually occurs before a consulting contract is agreed upon, but not always. Sometimes, no proposal is required; only a project plan is requested, along with project costs. Some proposals/contracts are very formal written documents that also include legal requirements, while other contracts are more informal, even simple verbal agreements with some working documents that are really outlines of the plan. However, every project requires that the client and consultant agree on the project's purpose, strategy, deliverables, and more. The basic elements of proposals/contracts are described below, with sample proposals on the pages that follow:

Introduction
This is an expression of your desire to do the work and may be part of an email (with the proposal as an attachment), a cover letter (if mailed or faxed), or just a verbal statement.

Project purpose
This includes overall purpose and specific project goals. This enables the client to realize that you understand the full intention of the project.

Project strategy
This explains the overarching strategy for (the approach to) the work and should (a) align with the purpose and (b) create the framework for the deliverables and the tactics.

Project deliverables
This describes exactly what you will produce.

Project roles
This states your understanding of your role, the client's role, and others' roles as appropriate.

Resources
This includes your time and the time of others, logistics such as meeting room or audiovisual requirements, materials, and/or other communication or administrative needs.

Time frame
This involves a time frame for completing the entire engagement, as well as the time being broken down for specific deliverables and milestones, if known.

Fees and expenses
Fees may be based on the number of consulting days, a fixed project fee, or some other compensation structure such as a retainer. Expenses include any out-of-pocket expenses such as travel, meals and hotel, materials, etc.

Credentials and experience
This involves relevant credentials and experience for doing this particular kind of work and references, if requested (name, organization, role, email, and phone number). Be careful to protect the anonymity of past clients. If giving references, let references know you have done so in advance, even asking their permission.

Next steps
This offers suggestions for moving forward and what you will do once the work is approved. This step can be in an email, cover letter, or verbally.

PROJECT PROPOSAL 1

For: XXXXX
Consultant: Ginger Lapid-Bogda
Company: The Enneagram in Business
Date: XXXXX

Project Outline

Purpose: To design and deliver a 1-day team development program focused on the Enneagram and how to use it to lead high-performing teams, take charge of change, and partner strategically with customers.
Steps: Determine goals and design process for session and deliver the 1-day program.
Delivery Date: XXXXX

Estimated Project Cost: XXXXX

Consulting: XXXXX
   Ginger Lapid-Bogda:
   Planning: 4 hours @ XXXXX per hour = XXXXX; Delivery: 1 day offsite @ XXXXX per day = XXXXX
Travel: XXXXX
   Hotel: XXXXX
   Airfare: XXXXX
   Food: XXXXX
   Cabs: XXXXX
Materials: XXXXX
7 tools for 10 participants = 70 tools @ XX per tool = XXXXX

Consultant Information

Contact
Address | 310.829.3309 (o) | 310.829.3386 (f)
TheEnneagramInBusiness.com | ginger@TheEnneagramInBusiness.com

Background
Ginger Lapid-Bogda, Ph.D. is an internationally recognized Enneagram author, teacher, and keynoter as well as an organizational consultant, trainer, and coach for Fortune 500 companies, service firms, government agencies, and non-profits. Her company, The Enneagram in Business, helps individuals and organizations use the Enneagram system for success in their personal and professional lives. Ginger is the author of *Bringing Out the Best in Yourself at Work*, *What Type of Leader Are You?*, *Bringing Out the Best in Everyone You Coach*, *The Enneagram Development Guide*, and *Consulting with the Enneagram*. She conducts Train-the-Trainer and ICF approved coaching certificate programs around the world, provides state-of-the-art training tools, an Enneagram eLearning Portal, and the Enneagram App, *Know Your Type*.

PROJECT PROPOSAL 2

For: XXXXX
Consultant: Ginger Lapid-Bogda
Company: The Enneagram in Business
Date: XXXXX

Project Outline

Purpose: To design and deliver a 2-day program team development and leadership transition offsite that enables the XYZ current team, currently led by XXX, to effectively and seamlessly transition from their current leader to their new leader, YYY. Using the Enneagram combined with theory, models, and practice from leadership, leadership transitions, and high performance teams, the program will focus on in-depth individual and team effectiveness, leadership transition, and anchoring the leadership change.

Steps: Determine goals and design process for offsite; review plan with XXX and, later, YYY; meet with the two leaders to prepare for offsite; participate in pre-offsite dinner; deliver 2-day transition offsite.

Delivery Date: XXXXX

Estimated Project Cost: XXXXX

Consulting: XXXXX
   Ginger Lapid-Bogda:
   Planning: 1 day @ XXXXX = XXXXX; Delivery (includes 2 days offsite and 1 pre-day meeting with XXX and YYY):
        3 days @ XXXXX per day = XXXXX

Travel: XXXXX
   Hotel and Airfare: XXXXX
   Food: XXXXX
   Cabs: XXXXX

Consultant Information

Contact
Address | 310.829.3309 (o) | 310.829.3386 (f)
TheEnneagramInBusiness.com | ginger@TheEnneagramInBusiness.com

Background
Ginger Lapid-Bogda, Ph.D. is an internationally recognized Enneagram author, teacher, and keynoter as well as an organizational consultant, trainer, and coach for Fortune 500 companies, service firms, government agencies, and non-profits. Her company, The Enneagram in Business, helps individuals and organizations use the Enneagram system for success in their personal and professional lives. Ginger is the author of *Bringing Out the Best in Yourself at Work*, *What Type of Leader Are You?*, *Bringing Out the Best in Everyone You Coach*, *The Enneagram Development Guide*, and *Consulting with the Enneagram*. She conducts Train-the-Trainer and ICF approved coaching certificate programs around the world, provides state-of-the-art training tools, an Enneagram eLearning Portal, and the Enneagram App, *Know Your Type*.

PROJECT PROPOSAL 3

For: XXXXX
Consultant: Ginger Lapid-Bogda
Company: The Enneagram in Business
Date: XXXXX

Project Outline

Purpose

To inspire, inform, and generate action among the participants about how to use the Enneagram system of personality to enhance their own professional growth as well as the development of individuals, teams, and leaders in their local organizations.

The program will cover the following: Enneagram system; identification of Enneagram type; and applications of Enneagram to the work environment in areas such as communication, feedback, leadership, and teams.

Steps

Design the one-day program based on dialogue with XXX

Review design with XXX

Make revisions as needed

Deliver program at XYZ company

Program Date: XXXXX

Project Cost: XXXXX

Project Rate: XXXXX This project rate includes design and delivery of the one-day program, all training materials, and some expenses (airfare, cabs, incidental food costs); hotel costs and onsite food will be paid for by XYZ.

Consultant Information

Contact

Address | 310.829.3309 (o) | 310.829.3386 (f)

TheEnneagramInBusiness.com | ginger@TheEnneagramInBusiness.com

Background

Ginger Lapid-Bogda, Ph.D. is an internationally recognized Enneagram author, teacher, and keynoter as well as an organizational consultant, trainer, and coach for Fortune 500 companies, service firms, government agencies, and non-profits. Her company, The Enneagram in Business, helps individuals and organizations use the Enneagram system for success in their personal and professional lives. Ginger is the author of *Bringing Out the Best in Yourself at Work*, *What Type of Leader Are You?*, *Bringing Out the Best in Everyone You Coach*, *The Enneagram Development Guide*, and *Consulting with the Enneagram*. She conducts Train-the-Trainer and ICF approved coaching certificate programs around the world, provides state-of-the-art training tools, an Enneagram eLearning Portal, and the Enneagram App, *Know Your Type*.

PROJECT PROPOSAL 3 | "Something Cool" | Hiring Process Proposal

Purpose: To create an involving, exciting, and clarifying hiring process that allows XXXX to select the best hires in a short period of time, hires who work effectively in teams and are sufficiently aligned with the culture and a new way of teaming so that they can ramp up immediately, thus adding to the productivity and excellence of the organization in a short period of time

Strategy: To create a winnowing funnel of potential candidates through an assessment center-like process through which individual candidates and teams can continuously opt out of the process, with the result that the final teams are composed of people who truly want to work for the organization and XXXX can select from among the best pool of teams

Deliverables: To design and deliver a viable, fun, interactive, efficient, and effective process for (1) the 2-day hiring event; (2) the Monday evening large group event; (3) the assessor training event to train organizational staff how to evaluate teams for hire; and (4) the Saturday evening assessor review event

Roles: Ginger Lapid-Bogda will be the lead consultant bearing full responsibility for the design and delivery of this project as well as all client interface and the hiring and supervision of additional Enneagram-business consultants who will support this effort. The organizational project manager will interface with other vendors, company projects teams, and work collaboratively with Ginger on the design of this project.

Resources: Ginger will be responsible for securing all resources for the delivery of the event except technical support, AV, food and room arrangements.

Time frame: The time frame will be set by the client; the consultants will meet the needed schedule as long as there is sufficient advance notice.

Fees and expenses: These are included in a separate document.

Credentials and experience: These are included in a separate document.

PROJECT COST | "SOMETHING COOL"

For: XXXXX
Consultant: Ginger Lapid-Bogda
Company: The Enneagram in Business
Date: XXXXX

Overview

This budget covers both a 1-day Enneagram program (a customized pilot program) focusing on the Enneagram applied to communication, teams, and relationship development, and an innovative hiring process for XXX that requires extensive design and delivery. The 1-day training is scheduled for XXXX. The XXX project was scheduled for the week of XXXX, but is being rescheduled for late XXXX 2012.

Estimated Project Cost

Consulting Fees: XXXXX
    Ginger's Consulting Fees (delivery): 5 days @ XXXXX per day = XXXXX
    Ginger's Design fees: 6.5 days @ XXXXX per day = XXXXX
    Additional consultants for both projects (10 days-their prices vary) = XXXXX

Materials Fees: XXXXX
Includes both training tools for participants and customized materials

Travel Fees: XXXXX
Includes travel, hotel, and food for Ginger as well as other consultants

Total for PO: XXXXX
Summary of all items above

Consultant Information

Contact
Address | 310.829.3309 (o) | 310.829.3386 (f)
TheEnneagramInBusiness.com | ginger@TheEnneagramInBusiness.com

Background
Ginger Lapid-Bogda, Ph.D. is an internationally recognized Enneagram author, teacher, and keynoter as well as an organizational consultant, trainer, and coach for Fortune 500 companies, service firms, government agencies, and non-profits. Her company, The Enneagram in Business, helps individuals and organizations use the Enneagram system for success in their personal and professional lives. Ginger is the author of *Bringing Out the Best in Yourself at Work*, *What Type of Leader Are You?*, *Bringing Out the Best in Everyone You Coach*, *The Enneagram Development Guide*, and *Consulting with the Enneagram*. She conducts Train-the-Trainer and ICF approved coaching certificate programs around the world, provides state-of-the-art training tools, an Enneagram eLearning Portal, and the Enneagram App, *Know Your Type*.

CHAPTER 4
COLLECTING | CONSULTING with THE ENNEAGRAM

It requires a very unusual mind to undertake the analysis of the obvious.
Alfred North Whitehead

Collecting and analyzing data effectively takes curiosity, skills, objectivity, diagnostic ability, interpersonal sensitivity, and intuition. The following materials offer some guidance in doing all of these things:

Collecting and the Enneagram

Data-collection methods

Diagnostic framework methods

Structuring data-collection questions

Effective interviewing

Focus group guidelines

Data analysis

Post-collecting checklist

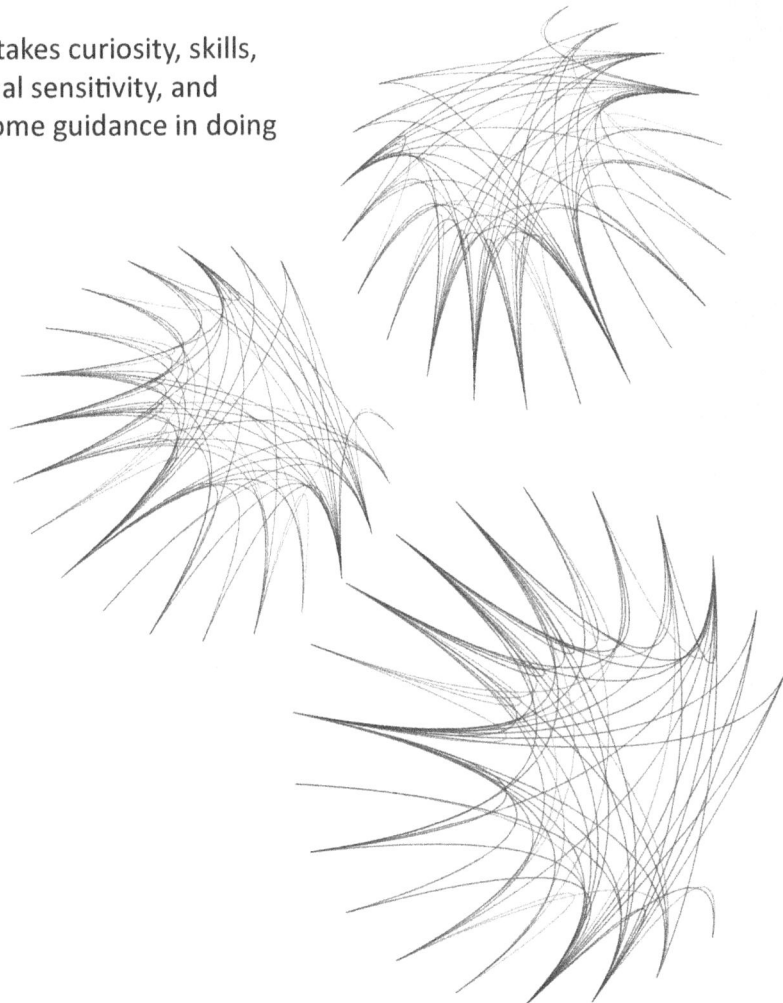

Collecting and the Enneagram

BODY

6. Closing

5. Changing

1. Contracting

4. Challenging

2. Collecting

3. Communicating

HEAD

HEART

What information will need to be collected in relation to the client's goals and desired outcomes?

Who has or where is this information?

What is the most effective, efficient, and comprehensive data-collection methodology?

When and how will this data be collected?

How will the data be analyzed?

Who will see the information (and in what sequence)?

Collecting refers to gathering objective and useful organizational information that will be instructive to the client. Many consultants gather consulting information only from the person to whom they are consulting. Although consultants may think they have good reasons for doing this, the drawback to this method is straightforward – we do not see ourselves in an unbiased way. We tend to perceive ourselves according to our intentions rather than our actual behavior, and we often emphasize the parts of ourselves that make us the hero of the story rather than the villain. When we have disagreements with others, most of us end up in our own minds as the victim, not the perpetrator.

The inability to appreciate our positive qualities may also hamper our ability to perceive ourselves objectively. Most people underestimate the importance of their strengths and overemphasize the areas in which they feel less capable. It is also common for people to have difficulty accepting positive feedback; some individuals actually prefer negative feedback to positive. In addition, we often take our strengths for granted and focus instead on what we perceive to be our deficits. Thus, it is extremely important to gather information from multiple sources *in addition* to collecting data directly from the person who is the client; this way, a balanced and realistic perspective is achieved.

Many avenues exist for collecting additional data, including confidential interviews (superiors, peers, subordinates, clients, vendors), surveys, prior performance reviews, videotapes, audiotapes, written communications (emails, reports), and direct observations (sitting in on meetings, watching presentations). An invaluable source of data is the consultant's direct experience with the client; real-time data directly from the consultant, particularly when the consultant has no perceived bias, often has a strong impact on the client.

Most clients want to know how they are perceived; simultaneously, they are often quite nervous during the data-collection phase. The following worries are both common and normal:

Will there be a stigma attached to using a consultant, such as others thinking there is something wrong with me?

Will people being interviewed or surveyed be forthcoming?

Will stories be fabricated about me?

Will the consultant delve into areas that should be avoided?

Will the data be collected and analyzed in an objective way?

Will the consultant, who is now my ally, begin to perceive me negatively if he or she hears or observes information contrary to what I've said during the consulting meetings?

Will the consultant say or imply anything negative about me to someone else?

These and other questions may be going through the client's mind during the data-collection phase. In order to assuage most of these concerns, it is helpful for the consultant to collaborate with the client regarding the following:

What questions will be asked

Who will contribute to the data

The method of collecting the data

The timing of data collection

How the data will be analyzed

Collaboration can take different forms – for example, the client may review the consultant's ideas, the consultant may refine ideas developed by the client, or the consultant and client can design the data-collection process together.

Additional issues often arise at the *Collecting* Stage of consulting that have to do with the client's trust in the consultant to honor the confidentiality agreements and to act in ways that help and do not hurt the client. Dealing with these delicate concerns directly actually fosters trust in the consulting relationship. For example, the consultant can say, "When asking for information, there will always be both positive and negative data. We'll use the information collected in a constructive way," and "When I ask questions during data-collection interviews, I merely seek information and do not give my opinion." A recommitment to the earlier confidentiality agreements also helps – "The only people who will see the data collected are the ones we discussed in our initial agreement." In addition, when collecting data, it is always advisable to ask questions that elicit both positive and negative responses. This not only makes the client feel less apprehensive, it also provides more balanced data about how the client is perceived. For example, a request such as, "Please describe this person's leadership style" can be followed up with these questions:

  What are this person's greatest leadership strengths?

  What are this person's key areas needing development?

Finally, the ability to maintain the anonymity of those who give data is crucial to the trust between the consultant and client. When anonymity has been promised to those from whom data has been collected, it is essential to honor this. If a consultant breaks this agreement and reports who said what, the consultant has not only breached the confidentiality of the person surveyed, but trust between consultant and client has also been called into doubt. The client will likely think: *If the consultant would breach someone else's confidentiality, how can I assume the same won't be done to me?*

Enneagram Insights

HEAD CENTER | ANXIETY AND FEAR

Although all consulting clients will have some concerns about trustworthiness of both the consultant and the data-collection process, individuals of the Head Center styles – Five, Six, and Seven – may have more anxiety about the trust between the consultant and themselves, as well as more fear about the rigor and accuracy of the data collected, than do individuals from the other two Centers. To help calm the mental agitation of these clients, the consultant can contact the client periodically to provide updates about the progress of the consulting. This involves sharing current information about the *process* of the data collection – for example, "Ten of the sixteen people have been interviewed" – but *not* the content of what has been gathered. Revealing the information prematurely would not only risk providing incomplete or incorrect data, it could also send a Head Center client into an unnecessary frenzy of thoughts and mental analysis. Another advantage to having periodic conversations related to the process of data collection is that doing so provides opportunities for discussion of any additional issues that may be on the client's mind.

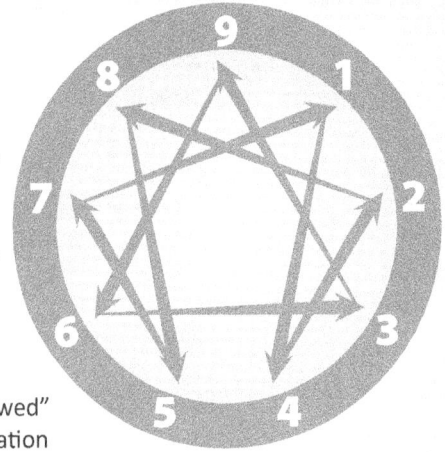

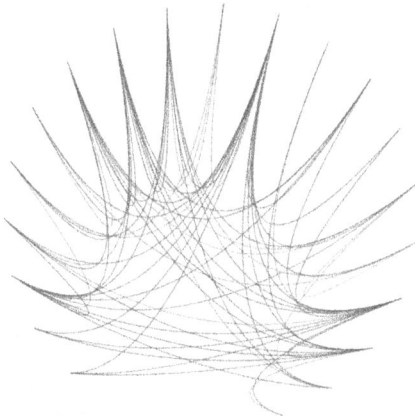

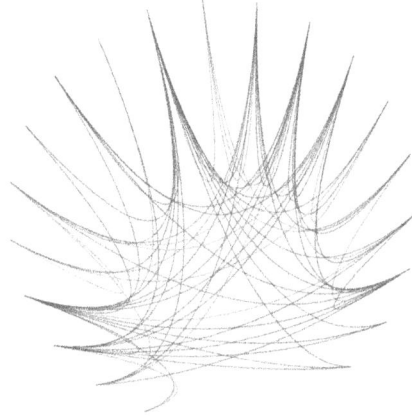

HEART CENTER | RELATIONSHIP

The quality of the relationship between the consultant and client is important to all consulting clients. However, when the consulting client comes from the Heart Center – styles Two, Three, and Four – he or she tends to pay even more attention to the relationship with the consultant, particularly during the time when the consultant is collecting information. Twos, Threes, and Fours will often read meaning into how the consultant acts when they are in direct contact, reading the consultant's body language, tone of voice, and other cues when they interact. The Heart Center styles tend to make the assumption that a positive attitude from the consultant toward them means that the consultant still thinks well of them, and that the data being collected thus can't be all that bad.

BODY CENTER | ACTION

Every consulting client hopes for a positive result from the consulting experience, although most clients will suspend judgment until they see the data during the *Communicating* Stage of the consulting. The Body Center styles – Ones, Eights, and Nines – tend to be more concerned than others at the *Collecting* Stage itself about whether positive action will come from the consulting. To reassure individuals with these styles, a simple and oft-repeated message suffices: "We're getting some very useful information that I think you'll find to be practical, balanced, constructive, and actionable." This message does need to be phrased in a way that is congruent with the consultant's language pattern and consistent with the emerging data, because the Body Center styles appreciate pure honesty. Consequently, if the emerging data seems to be more negative than positive, the word "balanced" might be misleading, and the word "honest" can be substituted.

Ones, Eights, and Nines do not share identical concerns regarding action. Ones like action that leads to improvement. However, they prefer their actions to be practical, logical, and concrete. With so many tasks already on their to-do lists, Ones want to be sure that what is going to be expected of them as a result of the data will be both worth the time *and* not overly time consuming. Eights tend to be more interested in whether the data will yield information that leads to high-impact action; they like big things to happen, and they prefer to not waste time on low-impact details. Nines are often interested in actionable areas that come from the data, but they will be more on guard than others against having too much action required of them, particularly if they do not want to do what the data suggests. Nines generally do not like being told what to do; consequently, they may perceive the forthcoming data as a demand for action. For Ones, Eights, and Nines, the consultant can offer reassurance that the client will be the one to choose what to change – not the consultant or anyone else. Once they believe this message, clients from the Body Center usually relax and even look forward to receiving data feedback during the next consulting stage.

Data-Collection Methods

To get the information needed, you have to select the best data-collection method for the particular project. Below are your choices, with two different ways to structure your questions on the following pages:

Methods	INTERVIEWS	QUESTIONNAIRES	DIRECT OBSERVATIONS	DOCUMENTS	GROUP MEETINGS (small and large)
	Individual Open-ended Semi-structured Structured	Standardized Modified from standard questionnaire Custom-made	Meetings Phone calls Walking around observing	360° feedback reports Internal, external documents Survey reports Performance reviews	Focus Groups Future Search Dannemiller Process Electronic Voting Open Space World Cafe
Advantages	Adaptive | data on large range of possible subjects including probes for more information Source of "rich" data, including qualitative information and comments Empathic | rapport-building	Quantifiable, easily summarized Useful with large numbers Relatively inexpensive Can obtain large volume of data Elicits data that client may not have been aware of	Behavioral data, not reports of behavior Real time, not retrospective Adaptive to changing situations Reveals data about which client-system may not be aware	Gives multiple perspectives Provides cognitive information Easy to identify gaps as well as strengths	Emergent Current Requires little consultant analysis Quick and in real-time Creates action Allows many people to have a voice
Potential Problems	Expensive Interviewer bias Coding and interpretation problems Self-report bias Restricted due to relatively small sample size	Non-empathic Predetermined questions may miss issues Misinterpretation Response bias Retrospective reporting Customized questionnaires hard to construct for validity and reliability Comments very difficult and time consuming to analyze	Interpretation and coding challenges Sampling bias | may be a one-time event and not a pattern Observer bias Expensive	Cool medium Information already filtered by document preparers Time consuming to review Conclusions limited to what documents reveal	Not anonymous Costly to create Consultant needs specialized skills Complex to set up Information very public Structure stifles conversation (in some groups)

Diagnostic Framework Questions

Vision and Mission | *What is the organization's vision, what business are you in, and how well are these aligned with your environment? To what extent are these shared throughout the organization?*

Strategy | *What are your key strategies for accomplishing your vision and mission, and how effective are they?*

Structure | *How are the work and tasks organized, and how effective is this in terms of achieving your strategies, mission, and vision?*

Rewards | *What rewards and incentives exist, are these aligned with the work that needs to be done, and do people care about them and perceive them as attainable?*

Processes | *What processes exist for communicating, coordinating, decision-making, and getting work done, and how effective are they?*

People | *Are the right people with the right skills in the right jobs, are they engaged and motivated, is their performance well-managed, how do organizational members get along, and how do people handle disagreements?*

Leadership | *What is the style of leadership, what are the leader's strengths and weaknesses, and what more (or less) could the leader do to provide direction and support?*

Culture | *What is the culture like, what are its values, and how would you describe the organization as a place to work?*

Vendors | *Who are your key suppliers or vendors and what are your relationships with them?*

Customers | *Who are your current and potential customers, and what do they think of you?*

The diagram on the left shows a vertical flow with downward arrows connecting: Vision & Mission → Strategy → Structure → Rewards → Processes → People → Leadership → Culture → Vendors → Customers

Structuring Data Collection Questions

In order to collect high quality, relevant data, you have to know the kind of information you need and get it from the right sources. Structuring questions is both a science and an art, and here are some ways to do this:

Use a relevant framework or model that relates to the data-collection query.

Ask questions clearly relevant to consultation goals and outcomes.

Ask questions in triangular form, from left to right, then to the bottom.

Current situation   Desired situation

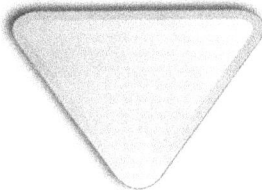

How to get there

Want more of...   Want less of...

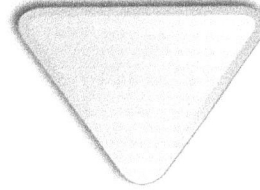

Want same of...

Strengths   Weaknesses

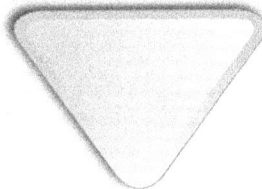

Neutral or mixed

Hopes   Fears

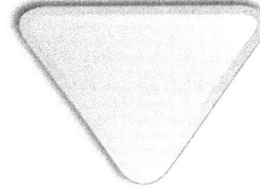

Opportunities

Works well   Needs work

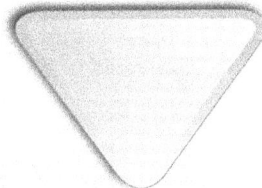

Need to create

Past   Present

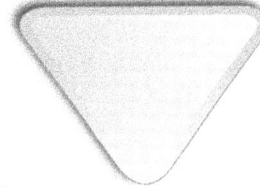

Future

The Steps of Effective Interviewing

Every consultant needs to know how to be an effective, objective interviewer. With practice, you'll get better and better.

Location
A number of factors enter into the ideal location: convenience, privacy, too large or too small a room, water or coffee available, temperature, tables large enough to write on but not so large as to create a barrier, comfortable chairs.

Comfort
It is the responsibility of the interviewer to put the interviewee at ease. There are many ways to do this, such as introducing yourself, offering them coffee, water, etc., reviewing the process, reassuring them of confidentiality, no tape recorders, good eye contact (even while taking notes), smiling, asking them if they have concerns or questions, really listening to them, comforting them if they are upset, being flexible so they can talk about things you have not asked about, thanking them at the end, etc. Do not tape record interviews; this makes interviewees suspicious.

Boundaries
This refers to all the things an interviewer does to keep the interview on track, such as starting and ending on time, letting the interviewee know how long the interview will last and how many questions will be asked, reviewing what will happen with the process after the interviews have been done, keeping track of time, and keeping their answers on track so all questions can be answered.

Questioning
While it is important that all the questions get asked in a similar way to all interviewees, it is equally important that the questions sound like they are coming naturally from the interviewer and not being read. To accomplish this, the interviewer needs to understand the intent of the question and also be able to ask the question in a few different ways. Keep questions open-ended and then probe for detail. Consider 5-7 questions for an hour interview. Begin with a "safe" question, and end with a question like "Anything else I need to know?"

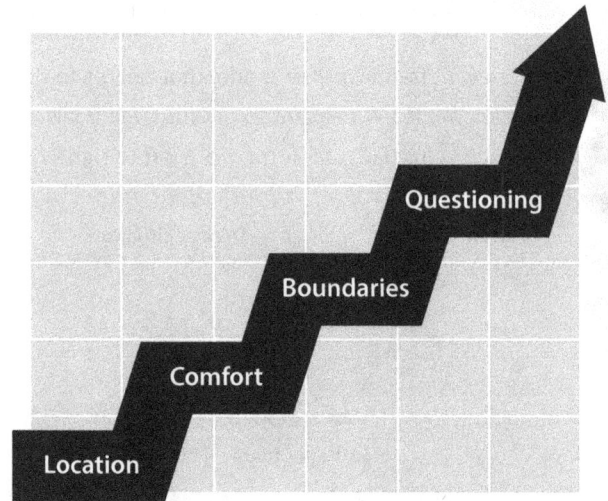

> **Data Collection Issues**
> What information should be gathered? | How will the data be gathered? | Who participates/how are they selected?

Focus Group Guidelines

Your data-collection methodology can include focus groups and individual interviews, focus groups and surveys, or just focus groups. These can be in addition to observed data as well as document reviews.

Pre-work

1. Organize the groups several weeks in advance; the participants should be selected at random, where possible.

2. Typically, you need to invite about 15 people to get 8; focus groups are ideally between 7-12 people. Fewer than 4 people should be individual interviews.

3. They need to RSVP; otherwise, you don't know whether you need to invite more people prior to the session.

4. Getting managers to tell people they need to attend increases the show rate dramatically.

5. Let them know, in writing, what the purpose of the meeting is but do not share the questions in advance.

Starting

1. Make sure you know how many people are supposed to be there; have access to someone who can call to see why people who RSVP'd are not there.

2. Start as close to the start time as possible (you can wait for no-shows up to 10 minutes).

3. Introduce yourself; have others introduce themselves.

4. Explain purpose and ground rules of the focus group:

   To gather data to give a snapshot of the organization in preparation for _____ (describe project)

   You will ask one question and anyone who wants to can respond; others can respond to a participant's response or respond directly to the question

   You may ask if others agree or not so you can get a sense of where the whole group stands on certain issues

   Confidentiality means you are looking for themes only; nothing that is said will be attributable to anyone by name or by event

   You will be taking notes

   They need to be confidential also; they are free to repeat anything they said and any themes but not any specifics that would attach any comments or events by someone else

Focus Group Guidelines

During the meeting

1. Takes notes verbatim (as much as possible).

2. Highlight important comments/ideas.

3. Take 100% verbatim notes on provocative/evocative comments.

4. If you don't understand something they say, ask a clarification question.

5. Don't take breaks.

6. Allot time so you cover all the questions (think about 1½-hour focus group as really 80 minutes of time).

Ending

1. Thank them for their comments.

2. Sometimes, at the end, someone says something significant; note it.

After the meeting

1. Review your notes; add elaborations of items you couldn't complete during the session.

2. Put your notes away and clear your mind for the next focus group.

3. Never tell one focus group what another focus group said.

Data Analysis

Taking data and transforming it into knowledge and insight for the client

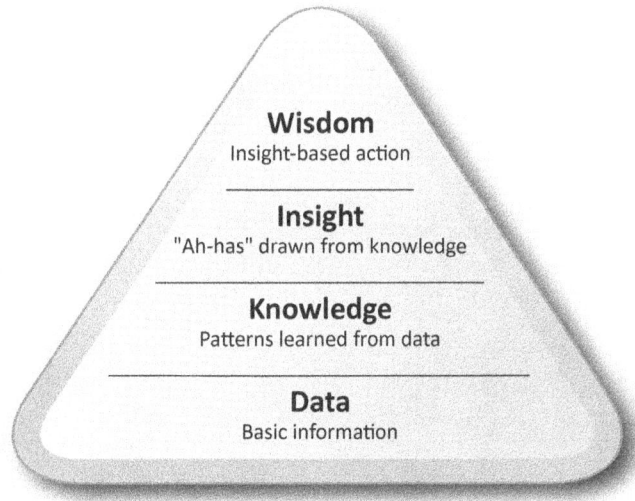

Wisdom
Insight-based action

Insight
"Ah-has" drawn from knowledge

Knowledge
Patterns learned from data

Data
Basic information

Data to Wisdom Pyramid

Purpose of Data Analysis

To stimulate the mind, evoke emotions, and propel the client toward intelligent action

Data

Relevant information (positive and negative) and new information (highlight the most important aspects)

Knowledge

Key issues (use frequency counts and anonymous, evocative quotes)

Gaps between what is the ideal situation (clearly stated and goal related)

Comparative data from groups (must have asked different groups the same question)

Insights

Root causes and other cause and effect relationships (must be able to perceive these relationships)

Frameworks that add perspective to the knowledge areas above (must use relevant frameworks that are appropriate for the sophistication level of client)

Wisdom is for the client to determine, not the consultant!

Post-Collecting CheckList

It is so important to do a post-consulting phase review to make sure that everything that needed doing was accomplished well and/or to identify areas that still need attention before moving forward in the consultation.

For each collecting topic below, rate yourself (3) well done; (2) needs more work; or (1) didn't do much and needs lots of attention. For items given a 1 or 2 rating, write down what you need to do prior to or during the next client meeting.

COLLECTING TOPIC	RATING	NEED TO DO
Data was collected in a coherent way (some theory-based framework or model used)		
Data was collected from a variety of relevant sources		
Data collection is complete according to the initial plan		
Discovered that more data would be helpful beyond initial plan		
Data collected lends itself to insightful analysis and diagnosis		
Data-collection process went smoothly		
Client seems satisfied with data-collection process thus far		
Consultant(s) satisfied with the data-collection process thus far		

CHAPTER 5
COMMUNICATING | CONSULTING with THE ENNEAGRAM

The single biggest problem in communication is the illusion that it has taken place.
George Bernard Shaw

Effectively communicating the data to the client in a way that is accurate, objective, impactful, diagnostic, sensitive, and compelling is a high standard. Yet, that is what needs to be accomplished during the Communicating Stage of the 6-C Consulting Model. Here are ways to help you do this:

Communicating with the Enneagram

Data presentation checklist

Sample of data presentation

Post-communicating checklist

Communicating and the Enneagram

BODY

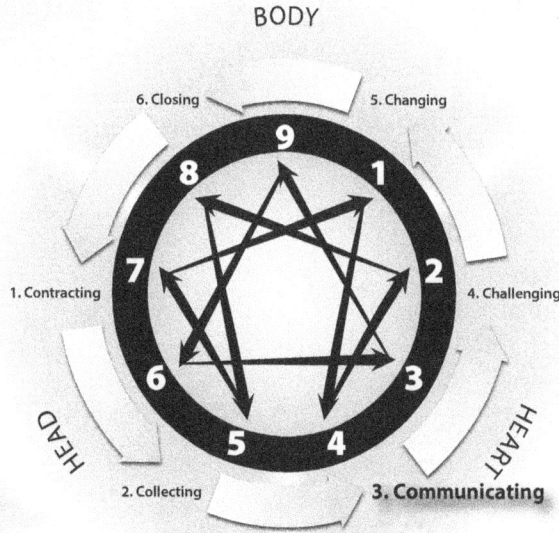

COMMUNICATING FOCUS AREAS

How will the data be organized in order to effectively communicate the core issues to the client?

What is the presentation strategy for the meeting with the client and others who need involvement?

When, where, and with whom will the data be shared?

What will be the structure and process of the data-feedback meeting(s)?

How will we move from understanding the data to the data's meaning (including diagnosis)?

Who will see the information (and in what sequence)?

How to Organize the Data

In order for the data to be communicated effectively to the client, it must first be organized. The most important criterion to consider is this: *What will have the most constructive impact on the client?* Because every situation is different, there is no single best way to organize data. However, the following factors need to be considered:

Quantity of data collected

Consistency of the data

Consulting goals

Client's learning style

The amount of time allotted to the meeting should not be a factor in determining how to organize the data; in fact, ample time should be prescheduled for the data-feedback meeting – a minimum of two hours, and as long as a full day.

Quantity of data collected

When a large quantity of data has been generated, the information needs to be crystallized down to a manageable size for the client. Few clients will be able to assimilate the equivalent of twenty or more pages of information; too much data can also cause the client and the consultant to lose their focus on the central themes that emerge. The most straightforward approach to honing the information is to organize it into main themes. It can also be helpful to have sub-themes and/or a sampling of quotes, listed anonymously and phrased in such a way that the identity of the person is not obvious.

Consistency of data

When the data itself is reasonably consistent, smaller amounts of information can be shared with the client because there is no need to overload the client with redundant information. With less consistent data, it is important to share more data and the nuances of the issues involved. For example, when the data reveals that a consulting client gives effective feedback but does so only intermittently, it serves the client well for him or her to know more information – for example, what precisely is meant by effective feedback, how often he or she is perceived as giving effective feedback, along with details regarding how often others need feedback from this individual and under what circumstances.

When the data is inconsistent and there is a wide range of perceptions, it is essential that even more data be communicated to the client. This data needs to include not only the full array of perceptions, but also some explanation for the spread of the responses.

Consultation goals

The consulting goals also influence the way in which the data is organized. Organizational models and other ways of grouping data that are relevant to the goals help to make the data more coherent. For example, if the client's goal is to become more influential in the organization and, specifically, to be promoted, the data can be organized around the specific skills required for that future position and the client's strengths and development areas compared to the requirements of that job.

Client's learning style

Once the consulting relationship has had time to develop, the consultant usually comes to understand the client's learning style and method of processing information. When the data is organized to complement the client's learning style, the impact will be far more powerful.

Here are some areas to consider. Most people learn best through one of three modalities: auditory, visual, or kinesthetic. Those with an auditory style prefer to hear information; visual individuals like to see it and often prefer pictures to words; kinesthetically oriented people learn best through experience. Consequently, auditory learners will want to hear *and* read the data. While visual learners may also want to read the data, they often prefer visually instructive charts, graphs, and pictures. As one such client pleaded, "Can you *please* draw me a picture of this so I can understand it?" For kinesthetic learners, the data should include anecdotes, stories, and quotes to put the information in terms of actual experience.

Verbal cues often indicate an individual's primary mode, and the most telling indicators are the nouns and verbs that person most commonly uses and the ways in which the person describes significant events. Following are three examples of a person describing the same successful work project using each of the three modalities described above.

AUDITORY

"I knew that the project was successful when I *heard* all the *feedback* from my boss. He *told* me that the clients *raved* about how well it had gone and would *call* us back when the next project comes up for bid."

VISUAL

"I knew that the project was successful when I *saw* the *look* on my boss's *face*. He *appeared* to be thrilled. In fact, he couldn't stop *smiling*. The client's reaction was better than anything I could have ever *pictured*."

KINESTHETIC

"I knew that the project was successful when my boss *came* to my office and *sat* down. He said that he had *made* the right decision by *putting* me on this project. The *sense* I got from him was that the client would *use* us again in a minute."

Those with an auditory mode tell us information through the use of verbs related to hearing. In contrast, the language of those with a visual mode is illustrated in word choices that are graphic and that imply the act of seeing. Last, kinesthetic language demonstrates how individuals with this preference frequently use action verbs or phrasing that suggests doing something.

If the primary learning and processing mode of the client is unknown, the best alternative is to organize the data so that it appeals to all three modes – *auditory*, *visual*, and *kinesthetic*. Most people have a secondary mode in addition to their primary one; consequently, a tri-modal approach usually reaches two of the three preferred learning styles of the client. Another method for helping to clarify the client's preferred mode is to ask the person directly. While clients may not relate to the words auditory, visual, and kinesthetic, they can usually answer the following question: "When you receive the data, do you have a preference for word summaries, pictures and graphs, or stories that describe the issues almost as if you had been there yourself?"

How to Conduct the Data-Feedback Meeting

The following agenda for the data-feedback meeting is divided into three parts: *Start-up*, *Discussion*, and *Closing*.

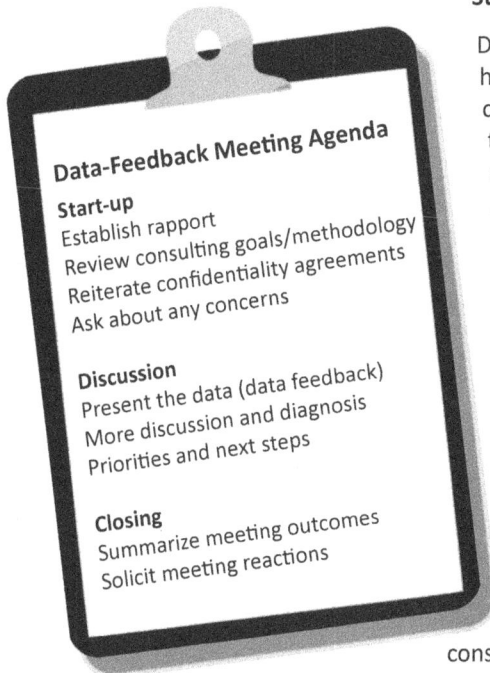

Data-Feedback Meeting Agenda

Start-up
Establish rapport
Review consulting goals/methodology
Reiterate confidentiality agreements
Ask about any concerns

Discussion
Present the data (data feedback)
More discussion and diagnosis
Priorities and next steps

Closing
Summarize meeting outcomes
Solicit meeting reactions

Start-up

During the data-presentation meeting, anxieties are usually high for both the consultant and the client. Although many consultants feel energized and excited at this phase, they typically have two primary worries: *(1) Is the data fair, accurate, and complete?* and *(2) Is the presentation of the data the best it can be in order to get the client's attention without unduly discouraging the client or damaging the consulting relationship?*

More often than not, the client is eager to hear the data but has mixed feelings. Clients often wonder: *Will the data be negative? Will I end up damaged personally or professionally? Will the consultant form a negative opinion of me? How should I handle myself during this meeting?* The items on the data-feedback meeting agenda are a sequence of topics that need to be discussed before any data is shared with the client. Discussing these items helps address the client's concerns so that their fears do not interfere with their ability both to hear the data accurately and to deal constructively with the information. The client is then ready to hear the data; in fact, delays in sharing the information can frustrate the client.

Discussion 1 | Present the data (data feedback)

Assuming that the data has been organized effectively as part of Stage 2, *Collecting*, the next challenge is to develop a strategy for presenting it. The successful execution of this strategy is pivotal to the success of the overall consulting. If the client does not understand and fails to internalize the key points from the data, or if he or she loses trust in the consultant as a result of reviewing the data – sometimes referred to as "killing the messenger" – a successful consulting relationship is likely to become derailed.

Some of the frequently asked questions about the data-sharing portion of the meeting include these:

Should a hard copy of the data be given to the client?

Should the data be given to the client all at once, or is it more effective to give the data to the client in distinct sections?

When is the best time for the discussion – after all the data has been presented, at key intervals, or when the timing just feels right?

The answers to these questions depend on a number of factors. Most consultants give their clients hard copies of the data, because clients like to refer to this information after the meeting. Even those of us who listen with a high degree of accuracy miss certain pieces of information. In stressful situations – and data-feedback meetings can feel stressful – people often forget exactly what has been said. The other rationale for providing the client with a hard copy of this data is that the data really belongs to the client, not the consultant. Under certain circumstances, however, not giving the client a hard copy of the information may be fine – for example, there may be a very small amount of data or the client doesn't want a hard copy.

Whether the consultant should give the client the data all at once or give the data out in distinct sections is a more complex issue. When sharing the data with the client, the consultant usually reviews the data verbally rather than having the client read the data silently. The verbal delivery is very important. It forces the client to keep pace with the consultant, rather than scanning the data and perhaps missing key issues. The consultant can also amplify what is written on the paper and also adjust his or her remarks in response to the client's questions and behavior. Most clients respect their consultants, and most want to understand the data as fully as possible. For these reasons, the client will usually follow the consultant's lead. When the consultant guides the client through information that has been gathered, it doesn't really matter whether or not the client has all of the data in his or her hands.

The main behavior to prevent is that of the client's reading through all the data on his or her own, without input from the consultant. If this happens, clients may draw premature and often incorrect conclusions. The consultant then has the double challenge of undoing the client's interpretations and refocusing him or her on the real meaning of the information. Handing out the data in smaller sections can prevent the client from going through the information prematurely, and most data falls into natural segments. Some clients, however, insist on having all of the data and reading through it by him or herself. In these cases, the consultant may decide that it is more important to have a client who is not angry than it is to be able to influence the client's initial interpretations of the information.

Discussion 2 | More discussion and diagnosis

In general, the optimal time for a discussion of the data is whenever either the client or the consultant wants to have one. The end of each natural section of information is an ideal time to ask the client a question such as "What do you think about this part of the information?" or "How did you react when you heard this?" Some parts of the data may contain more sensitive information – for example, information that conflicts with the client's self-perception or feedback that is critical. After the client has heard or seen this type of information, a question such as "How do you feel about what you've just heard?" or "What do you think about this?" can lead to productive discussions.

In addition, it is extremely important to solicit the client's reactions multiple times before the final discussion of the data. When clients do not speak during the feedback portion of the meeting, it often suggests that they are either unhappy with what they are seeing and hearing or are still thinking about something that was communicated earlier in the meeting.

It is important for the consultant to pay close attention to the client's reactions during the entire course of the meeting. The client's tone of voice or body language may change in noticeable ways – for example, the person may have a more subdued voice, a change in skin tone, or a furrowed brow. At these moments, an open-ended question such as "What are you thinking about?" is all that is needed to encourage the client to talk.

The most important discussion between the consultant and client comes after all of the data has been communicated and involves a forthright conversation about the meaning and implications of the information. The following two questions are an effective way for the consultant to initiate the conversation: "What in the data do you agree with?" and "What parts of the data do you disagree with or not understand?" After hearing the client's responses, it is helpful for the consultant to pursue those areas in which the client has questions or disagreements or does not understand something. It is helpful to pursue areas related to client questions and misunderstandings first. Depending on the issues raised, the consultant may offer additional insights or information. Alternatively, the consultant may ask, "What do you think this might mean?"

The final area to discuss involves the areas with which the client may disagree. Understandably, these are the areas that are the most likely to be emotion-laden for the client. During this part of the discussion, it is essential for the client to share both thoughts and feelings. A client may feel angry, hurt, or anxious about some of the feedback, and the consultant needs to understand his or her emotional frame of mind. Clients who hold in their anger or hurt often discount the data that has caused them to have this reaction. However, this may be exactly the information they need to understand and accept if they are to reach their consulting goals.

The most challenging part of the discussion for the consultant comes when a client strongly disagrees with something and has strong negative feelings about it. When this occurs, it is important for the consultant to draw out the client's reactions in some detail, using a comment such as "You seem to have a very strong reaction to this" or "Please tell me what is on your mind" to open the discussion.

The data with which a client disagrees can provide the basis for an effective consulting moment. There are several effective tactics for the consultant to use once he or she understands why the client disagrees with the information. When the client's disagreement comes from a lack of understanding of what the data means, the consultant can share information and perspectives that clear up the misunderstanding. When the client's difference in perception stems from a blind spot – that is, the client does not know that he or she does not know – the consultant can offer some feedback to the client, saying something such as, "I understand that you don't perceive yourself in this way; however, let me share my perceptions with you." An alternative approach is to ask the client both of the following questions: "If you don't think the data is accurate, please tell me what you think is correct from your perspective" and "Even if you think the data isn't accurate or fair, they are some people's perceptions. What do you think might cause someone else to have these perceptions?"

During all of the discussions in the *Communicating* phase of consulting, the consultant should feel free to share data collected in a form that will support the client's understanding of the issues and desire to take action, but also the consultant's perceptions, perspectives, and feedback. The challenge for most consultants is to develop the art of timing the delivery. Often, the best time for the consultant's input is after the client has shared his or her thoughts and feelings, because this allows the consultant to first hear and see the client's unfiltered responses; otherwise, clients may tailor their responses to coincide with what they believe the consultant wants to hear. On occasion, the consultant may want to say something before the client does – for example, to make a strong assertion, to highlight a perspective, or to share a personal experience.

Only after all the data has been shared, discussed and collectively understood by the client and consultant can an accurate and effective diagnosis of the "real" issues take place. Hopefully, the stage was set for the diagnosis as a result of the way the consultant organized the data itself. At the same time, new underlying issues, root causes and cause-effect understanding may have emerged during the discussion of the data. It is essential that the client and consultant both understand the true underlying causes of issues rather than mistaking the manifestations or symptoms of a problem for the real causes.

Discussion 3 | Logistics and next steps

Once the data has been discussed and a diagnosis has occurred, the next step is to prioritize the key areas needing the most attention. The consultant and client usually identify these issues collaboratively, and many criteria can be used to set priorities – for example, issues directly related to the consulting goals; root causes and critical themes that have urgency for the organization or the client; and areas that excite or distress the client. This is also the time to clarify the next steps for the consulting process. This includes when you will meet again after the client has had time to digest and process the data and its implications for change.

Closing

At the very end of the meeting, it is important to summarize what occurred, repeat the agreed-upon next steps, and to ask for reactions to the meeting, the data, and the plans. This allows everyone to have a voice and to hear whether or not there really is agreement to move forward. If there is not, obviously the areas where there is not agreement need to be addressed in order to proceed forward.

Task and Process Focus During Communicating (Data-Feedback Meetings)

During the data-feedback meeting, the consultant who is facilitating the conversation needs to pay attention to both the meeting task (the content) and the meeting process (communication, decision making, meeting tone and pace, feelings of participants), and to manage the balance between the task and the process. While task and process are important at all times during the meeting, at different intervals of stages either the task or the process becomes more important. The Feedback Meeting Sequence illustrates the shift in degree of task versus process focus.

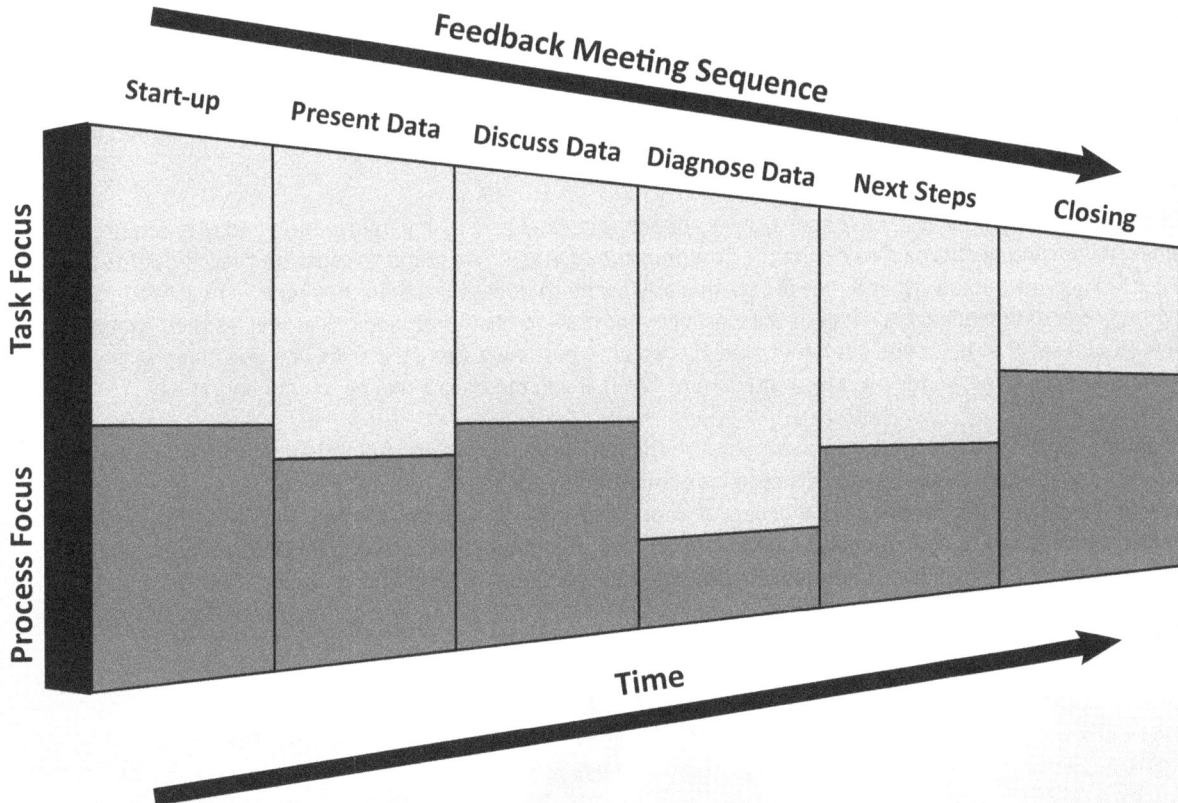

Enneagram Insights

HEAD CENTER | OVERANALYSIS

Enneagram styles Five, Six, and Seven typically respect data and prefer more data to less. They tend to analyze, challenge, and produce counterarguments, but they generally respond favorably to data that is logical, well organized, and thorough. Their tendency to question the data or the data-collection process does not necessarily mean that they do not agree with it. The Head Center styles seek to understand; part of the way they learn is through extensive mental processing.

When communicating data to Fives, Sixes, and Sevens, it is important that the consultant have anonymous anecdotes, quotes, or the consultant's direct observations to supplement the data that has been synthesized into key themes.
The reason for this is that some Fives, Sixes, and Sevens may use their own logic to invalidate the themes, to downplay their importance, or to discount the importance of perceptions in general. Because individuals from the Head Center tend to focus on the facts, they often need to have the associated feelings highlighted for them in an explicit way.

Fives, Sixes, and Sevens also have specific ways of analyzing and processing information and may require different consulting approaches during the *Communicating* Stage. Fives tend to separate their thoughts from their feelings automatically, and they are particularly prone to doing this when they receive negative information. When giving data feedback to Fives, it is especially important to elicit their feelings as well as their thoughts. If a Five should say that he or she has had no feelings about a particular item, the following question, delivered with humor, is often effective for opening a discussion: "Well, if you did have a feeling, what might it be?"

In addition, Fives may begin to compartmentalize the data they receive. In effect, they may hear one piece of information, place it in a category in their minds, and then move on to another piece of data without necessarily seeing the connection between the two sets of information. The consultant can help the Five client make these linkages by asking a simple question such as "Do you see the connection between this information and the earlier data?" or by making a statement that shows the direct relationship. For example, "The reason that people perceive your behavior in this way has to do with what we discussed in the earlier feedback. Does that make sense to you?"

Sixes are often quick to become worried and anxious both before the data presentation and during it. They may worry about what might happen, what is happening, and what has happened. They may also worry about worrying, wondering whether they are worrying too much or too little, or worrying about the right things. The

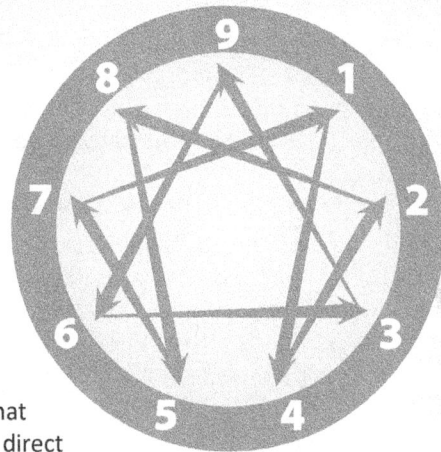

more the consultant maintains a calm demeanor and makes comments to assuage the Six's anxiety, the more the Six will be able focus on what is really being communicated during the meeting. Sometimes an early statement from the consultant helps, such as, "You may feel apprehensive about the information to be discussed; let me assure you that you have all the ability to work with anything negative, and that there is a great deal of positive data as well." Alternatively, the consultant can suggest, "Any time you have any concerns whatsoever, please bring them up and I'll help you with them."

Because most Sevens seek positive and pleasurable experiences and try to avoid situations in which they anticipate feeling uncomfortable, inadequate, or hemmed in, they rarely look forward to the data-feedback meeting. Some Seven clients will actually avoid meeting with their consultant once the data feedback is about to begin. That said, many Sevens do take their responsibilities seriously; for them, a scheduled meeting is a commitment.

When Sevens do cancel feedback meetings or show up late to them, it cannot be assumed that this is a conscious and deliberate act on their part. Sevens juggle so many balls in the air simultaneously that there is almost always some other person, meeting, or task demanding their attention. Avoiding the feedback session may be rationalized and reframed by Sevens as a situation in which another demand for their time was a higher priority. Consequently, the first challenge is to get Sevens both to be timely with their consulting appointments and to allow enough time in the meeting for a thorough discussion of the feedback.

To meet this challenge, the consultant must have patience, compassion, and clarity. Patience is required because Sevens may be late or miss their appointments multiple times. Compassion helps the consultant to become more patient; while outwardly Sevens may not appear to be afraid of what the data may indicate, they may actually be feeling extremely apprehensive. Clarity refers to the need for the consultant to be quite clear with the Seven about the value of the consultant's time and the impact of the Seven's lateness on both client and consultant.

During the session itself, Sevens like to see as much data as possible; in fact, they often process large amounts of information quickly. However, their interpretations of the data may not always be accurate. Therefore, it is important that the consultant elicit the Seven's thoughts and feelings about each piece of the information. When Sevens misinterpret data, it is frequently the result of one of the two ways in which they process information.

First, Sevens tend to reframe negative information in order to put it in a positive light. For example, a Seven may hear that he or she is perceived to complete projects with a flurry of activity at the very last minute, with the effect of creating undue stress and pressure on others. The Seven may reframe this feedback to mean that such behavior ensures quality control, since a project cannot be fully assessed for quality until all of the components have been put together. There is logic to this reframing that may, at first glance, appear difficult to refute. However, the consultant can also use the technique of reframing to help the Seven understand the true meaning of the data – for example, by adding the following perspective: "Let's examine a number of factors that determine quality such as clear project requirements, the skills of the project staff, appropriate work delegation, quality milestones at several intervals before project completion, *and* a quality check at the end of the project. Let's assess your behavior against all these quality-related factors." What the consultant is doing here is employing the Seven's own words (ensuring quality) and using them as the basis for the reframing.

The second way in which Sevens may discount data is to select certain pieces of information with which they disagree; in the Seven's mind, this implicitly calls into question the remaining data. For example, the data may suggest that the Seven needs to work on his or her ability to maintain confidential information. When the consultant gives only one example, the Seven may explain why this example is incorrect, thus denying that maintaining confidentiality is an issue. With Sevens, it is particularly helpful to have multiple examples of a key data point, as this will make it much more likely that the Seven will understand his or her patterns of behavior.

HEART CENTER | THE REACTIONS OF OTHERS

Twos, Threes, and Fours are the most likely to be concerned about how they are seen by others. When the consultant is communicating data, the Heart Center styles will want to learn as much as they can about how others perceive them. For example, they will often ask questions about how many people share a given perception, whether or not there is a wide range of perceptions, how intensely the perceptions are held, what in their behavior causes these perceptions, what the consequences are of others' having these perceptions, and what can be done to turn any negative perceptions around. When the consultant is prepared to address these concerns, communicating the data moves forward dramatically.

An incorrect inference might be made from the ideas in the above paragraph that reporting an abundance of information to individuals with Heart Center Enneagram styles contributes to the success of the consulting. In fact, it is often preferable to provide Twos, Threes, and Fours with less elaborate data in writing and to amplify the information verbally. Heart Center styles often absorb information more fully through discussion and interaction. In addition, their questions may be highly specific and may thus refer to areas not documented by the consultant in anticipation of the meeting.

There are additional reasons to use a concise and focused approach to data feedback when consulting Heart Center clients. Because Twos, Threes, and Fours tend to be concerned first and foremost with how others are reacting to them, they may feel confused by too much data and may wonder which pieces of information are the most important. In addition, they may focus intently on the perceptions of others, becoming so other-directed that they may lose sight of how they actually feel about the issues raised, how they perceive themselves in relation to these issues, and what consulting goals they still want to pursue. While it is important for every client to learn to accept and respond to feedback in a constructive way, it is equally important that the client not lose his or her sense of self in the process.

Although most people feel hurt – at least to some degree – when they receive negative feedback, Twos, Threes, and Fours tend to feel particularly hurt when they hear negative information, although Twos and Fours will show this more visibly than Threes. It is therefore important to make sure that the language used to report the data is stated in an objective, yet supportive way. For example, when the data refers to the manner in which individuals of these Enneagram styles display their anger, it is better to say, "When tense or stressed, you tend to appear more on edge or unpredictable in your anger" than it is to say, "When you're angry, everyone stays out of your way."

Twos, in particular, may have difficulty making the time for a data-feedback session; during data feedback, the focus is on the client, and Two clients can feel extremely uncomfortable paying this much attention to themselves. In addition, Twos often become so busy giving to others at work that their time is a scarce commodity, or they may be so overwrought with doing for others that they don't feel that they have the emotional reserves to deal with negative data about themselves. Finally, Twos like people to like them; the idea that they may hear something negative about themselves during a feedback meeting is thus very unappealing. However, Twos tend to keep their word, so if they commit to a feedback meeting, they can usually be counted on to appear.

An important question when consulting Twos is that of where to have the feedback session, because the setting of the meeting often contributes dramatically to its success. For Twos as well as for individuals of all Enneagram styles, it is preferable for the meeting to be held in a place where there are no distractions. This usually means outside of their office and in a location where no one will be able to overhear the conversation. With Twos, however, attention to the details of the setting is even more important. Because Twos often make an effort to please the other person and make him or her feel comfortable, they appreciate it when someone else takes the time to think about what *they* might want. When this occurs, Twos typically are more relaxed and a relaxed client is far more open to consulting.

There is no one setting that Twos prefer, but they may tell you what they like if they are asked. Many Twos respond well to a feedback meeting at an attractive restaurant that serves excellent food and has good acoustics. Other Twos may prefer the beach, the mountains, or the golf course. What matters most is to get Twos away from all the people at work who need them for a variety of reasons and into a context in which they are the primary focus.

Threes often look forward to feedback, particularly if the feedback both highlights their accomplishments and contains actionable information that will help them become even more successful. Because the word "failure" is often not in their vocabulary, Threes usually prefer feedback that is kind and straightforward.

Once Threes think they hear some of the data, they will often be ready to take action before the consultant has even completed sharing all the information. The challenge for the consultant is to help the Three slow down his or her pace and take some time to reflect, examining deeper feelings, before making a decision to change anything. An effective way to help Threes slow down their process is to simply make a comment such as, "Can you slow down before you consider what actions to take? Let's talk about how you really feel when you hear feedback like this."

It is worth pointing out something about Threes that may not be obvious to an observer. While Threes often have many friends, with these individuals perhaps having been in their lives for decades, Threes often have few true confidants – people in whom they confide their deepest feelings and concerns. There are two reasons for this: first, most Threes have extremely busy lives, thus leaving little time for the development of deeper relationships; second, they are frequently reluctant to share their deeper emotions, particularly those related to their self-perceived shortcomings and failures. The consultant often becomes a confidant and advisor to the Three – a surrogate friend – particularly if the Three respects the consultant and feels respected in return. Consultants who have this type of reciprocal relationship with a Three client are in a position to have an enormously positive impact.

Fours can vary in their reactions to data feedback, but almost all of them will be concerned at some level that the data will cause them to feel defective and rejected. Fours tend to internalize negative data about themselves, because they often lack effective filters to help them determine whether a negative perception is accurate. Fours tend to do the opposite with positive feedback; in this case, rather than internalizing what they hear, as they do with negative data, Fours tend to discount or downplay positive information. They may savor positive remarks momentarily, but then quickly discard the information without integrating any of it into their self-perception. Because of this automatic injection or rejection pattern with feedback, Fours often need the consultant to help them sort out the truth and accuracy of the information presented.

Fours may prefer consultants who are sympathetic and understanding; however, what helps them grow the most are consultants who are warm, yet objective and direct. Because most Fours tend to feel hurt and rejected when they feel criticized, they may miss a kernel of insight or overlook the bigger picture of what has been said. For example, when the data says, "This leader inspires the best in people; at times, more attention could be focused on the underperformers," a Four might interpret the data to mean, "I am not a good leader because I don't inspire *everyone* to achieve excellent performance." A consultant can point out that this interpretation is taking a primarily positive idea and placing undue emphasis on the negative component. This can be particularly helpful when the consultant also highlights that this focus on the negative – that is, on what is missing – is part of the Four's pattern of processing information.

Fours may not always like hearing it, but they do appreciate being told the truth. Sometimes the truth may be far more positive than the Four's perception, and at other times it may be more negative. Deep inside, most Fours know that they can lose a balanced perception of reality and may need to rely on someone else's input in order to regain the bigger view. A trustworthy consultant is in an ideal position to offer this type of assistance. The proper timing is essential. The optimal moment for discussing negative data is directly after the Four client has expressed his or her feelings and perceptions about the information; at this time, the Four is usually quite receptive to what the consultant has to offer, as long as it is said with kindness.

BODY CENTER | HONESTY AND CLEAR ACTION

Individuals from the Body Center – Ones, Eights, and Nines – like honest, practical data that implies clear action. Body Center styles instinctually sense honesty in others; this sense is usually more visceral than cognitive or emotional. Therefore, the data needs to be straightforward and "unsanitized." In the behavioral sciences, "sanitized" refers to data that has been reworked to eliminate strong, controversial, or offensive data. Because sanitized data is often ambiguous or muted, its use would interfere with the consulting process when the client is a One, Eight, or Nine. In addition, because the Body Center styles have a tendency to use the defense mechanism of denial when they hear or experience something they find unpleasant, it is especially important to make certain that they actually hear the real message. This needs to be accomplished through repetition or emphasis rather than force. Individuals from the Body Center must also feel that the action decided upon is their choice as control is a central issue for these three styles.

Ones, Eights, and Nines also react very differently during data feedback. Ones usually prefer many details and concrete examples when they receive feedback. They tend to work from the specifics in order to understand the larger picture; consequently, they find tangible information to be quite useful. In addition, the more the data demonstrates cause and effect, the more positively Ones respond to it. For example, when the data says that the individual "needs to delegate work more effectively," Ones usually need to understand exactly what is meant in precise and practical terms. Here are some details that might appeal to Ones: "If you want to learn how to delegate most effectively – as opposed to doing all the work yourself or handing off tasks to someone, hoping that he or she will follow-through – here are some practical ideas. You can set up a series of meetings to accomplish the following: discuss project goals for each individual; provide in-person progress checks at regular intervals; and review all work with the entire team one week prior to the completion date. These checkpoints would both empower team members to do more independent work and simultaneously assure quality control."

Ones embrace improvement and appreciate ideas for achieving it. Simultaneously, they are very sensitive to feeling criticized and can often react to neutral statements as though these were criticisms. In addition, many Ones can't help but notice mistakes, and they are more prone to doing so when they feel stressed or anxious. For these reasons, it is very important to make certain that a data-feedback report, if there is one, contains no errors in grammar or punctuation, and certainly no typographical errors. When Ones read a poorly executed document, this can raise doubts in their minds regarding the accuracy of the content. It is not uncommon for Ones to take a pen to the page of a feedback report and edit the document as they read it.

The content of the report must also contain no inaccuracies. When a story is used as an example, the facts need to be right. The choice of words must also meet the One's standard of precision and accuracy; otherwise, a dispute about a nuance of meaning may occur. For example, when the feedback describes a One's behavior in a meeting by saying, "She began doing work in the middle of the meeting," a One might take offense at this comment and say, "I wasn't doing work. I was taking notes. You have it all wrong." While this reaction may actually give the consultant some excellent material for giving the One feedback about his or her right-wrong thinking process, the consultant may not want to elicit this type of response from the client at this time. A simple change in the way in which the data is worded will get a far more positive response from a One. For example, "It was perceived that you began doing work in the middle of the meeting," is not precise enough for Ones. It is more effective to say, "You began writing during the middle of the meeting, and this was perceived by some team members as your not being engaged in the conversation."

Finally, Ones often act quickly; they are usually busy, wanting to get things fixed and to clear their to-do lists. A consultant can support One clients by helping them identify multiple courses of action rather than an immediate "best" one, encouraging them to take the time to consider other possibilities. Some Ones may resist this idea because they feel so relieved when they complete tasks, but taking the time to contemplate and deliberate can be invaluable. One way for the consultant to encourage this behavior is to say to the One, "Your ideas are excellent, and there are certainly others that we have not considered yet. It would be unfortunate to make the wrong choice by deciding too early. Waiting only a few days or even a week often leads to the best course of action."

Eights usually like their data to include the biggest picture possible, with details used as supporting documentation. Eights often prefer this approach because they seek to understand the core issues and the overall patterns before they focus on the details. In addition, they do not like to waste time; going over what they consider to be minutiae can be highly annoying. As an Eight client once said, "Just give it to me!"

While many Eight clients make strong statements similar to the one above, beneath their bold exteriors they are usually feeling just as concerned and vulnerable as do individuals of all other Enneagram styles. However, at first Eights tend not to show this side of themselves, even when they respect and trust the consultant. Still, they will often open up after just a short time; particularly if the consultant asks them a question immediately after presenting some data that the Eight may have found troubling. For example, feedback such as, "He is a warm and sensitive person who goes out of his way to help others succeed," can unnerve an Eight, who, while feeling the information to be true, may also have believed that this attribute was not obvious to others. The reason for the discomfort is that being perceived in a highly positive way can make many Eights feel vulnerable, and they may even get misty-eyed. A question from the consultant such as, "Are you aware that others appreciate you in this way?" can illicit a wide range of unexpected emotional responses from an Eight.

Eights are also prone to taking action immediately upon hearing the data. While this may sound similar to the behavior of Threes, Eights often want to take big, bold, and decisive action, whereas Threes tend to be more focused on specific goals and systematic, incremental steps. The Eight's response is also different from the quick action of most Ones, who will focus more on specific tasks and the details of implementation. Eights will tend to create a large game plan of action on their own, but it may be one that is too far-reaching to achieve in a reasonable period of time. On other occasions, the Eight may not know what to do and will say to the consultant, "Tell me what to do!" In either case, the consultant can help the Eight most by helping him or her to slow down, to consider the data from many perspectives, and to develop a manageable action plan after having taken sufficient time to reflect on the meaning of the data and all of the options for action.

Some Eights may feel angry when they hear feedback; in these situations, the most helpful way to respond is to let them fully express their feelings. Once Eights have purged themselves of these intense reactions, they are usually ready to talk; very often, the Eight's post-anger period provides a valuable consulting opportunity. The consultant can help the Eight explore a wide range of thoughts, feelings, and behaviors by using supportive and direct questions or comments, such as these:

"What about this causes your strong reaction?"

"Tell me more about how you typically react in these situations."

"When you have these reactions, what else is also going on inside you?"

Nines usually prefer data that includes a great deal of detail and demonstrates multiple perspectives and interpretations of the key themes. Because Nines like concrete action, they appreciate data they can grasp readily. Instead of preferring to get the big picture alone first, they often like to integrate the big picture and the details simultaneously. When the data indicates that the Nine "needs to move projects along more quickly," it is helpful to include information that acknowledges the variety of reasons why this may not be occurring – for example, work overload, late hand-offs from coworkers, unclear directions from the Nine's boss – as well as the exact behavior of the Nine that contributes to the problem. After receiving specific information, Nines appreciate an explanation of the bigger impact of the issue – for example, loss of clients or conflict with other work units.

Almost all Nines need to feel rapport with the consultant before they are ready to hear constructive feedback. Nines typically seek a feeling of harmony with others under normal circumstances; in situations where Nines are under stress such as the anticipation of negative information about themselves, the consultant can help the Nine feel more relaxed by taking extra time at the start of the meeting to have a casual and engaging conversation about a topic of mutual interest. The challenge for the consultant is to make sure that sufficient time remains to do the work of communicating the data.

Consultants can also provide valuable assistance to the Nine client during the prioritizing phase of the data-feedback meeting. Difficulty with prioritization is a key issue for most Nines; consequently, while the last phase of the data-feedback meeting can be challenging for Nines, it also presents a significant learning opportunity for them. The consultant can help the Nine client the most not by prioritizing the issues for him or her, but rather by guiding the client through the process of thinking through the prioritization criteria and then helping the Nine to make a decision about which issues are really the most important ones.

Data Presentation: Criteria Checklist

Format

Is the data easy to read? Yes _____ No _____
If no, what would improve it?

Is the format pleasing to the eye? Yes _____ No _____
If no, what would improve it?

Is the format logical (mentally, emotionally, and from an action perspective)? Yes _____ No _____
If no, what would improve it?

Overall Content

Does the data tell the complete story? Yes _____ No _____
If no, what appears to be missing?

Does the data evoke a desire to act or to change something? Yes _____ No _____
If no, what would help?

Specific Content

Are there core themes and are they coherent? Yes _____ No _____
If no, what would make sense?

Are the quotes evocative and illustrative? Yes _____ No _____
If no, what would help?

Are the themes and quotes sequenced appropriately (similar ones together, redundancies eliminated, contrasting ones juxtaposed)? Yes _____ No _____
If no, what would you change?

Analyses

Is the information primarily at the knowledge and insight level? Yes _____ No _____
If no, what should be changed?

Is a framework used to help the data make sense? Yes _____ No _____
If no, what could you use?

Does the data include a way of diagnosing or analyzing the issues? Yes _____ No _____
If no, what could you add?

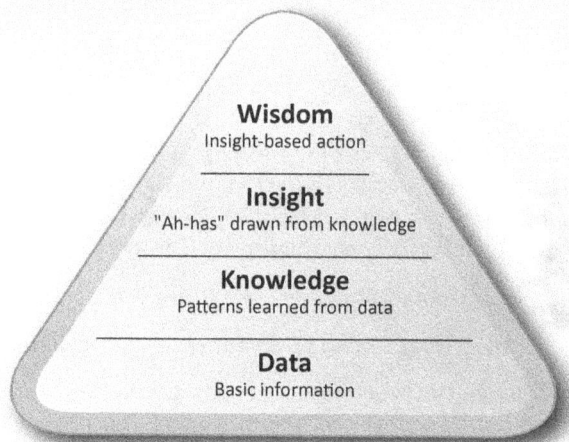

Wisdom
Insight-based action
_____

Insight
"Ah-has" drawn from knowledge
_____

Knowledge
Patterns learned from data
_____

Data
Basic information

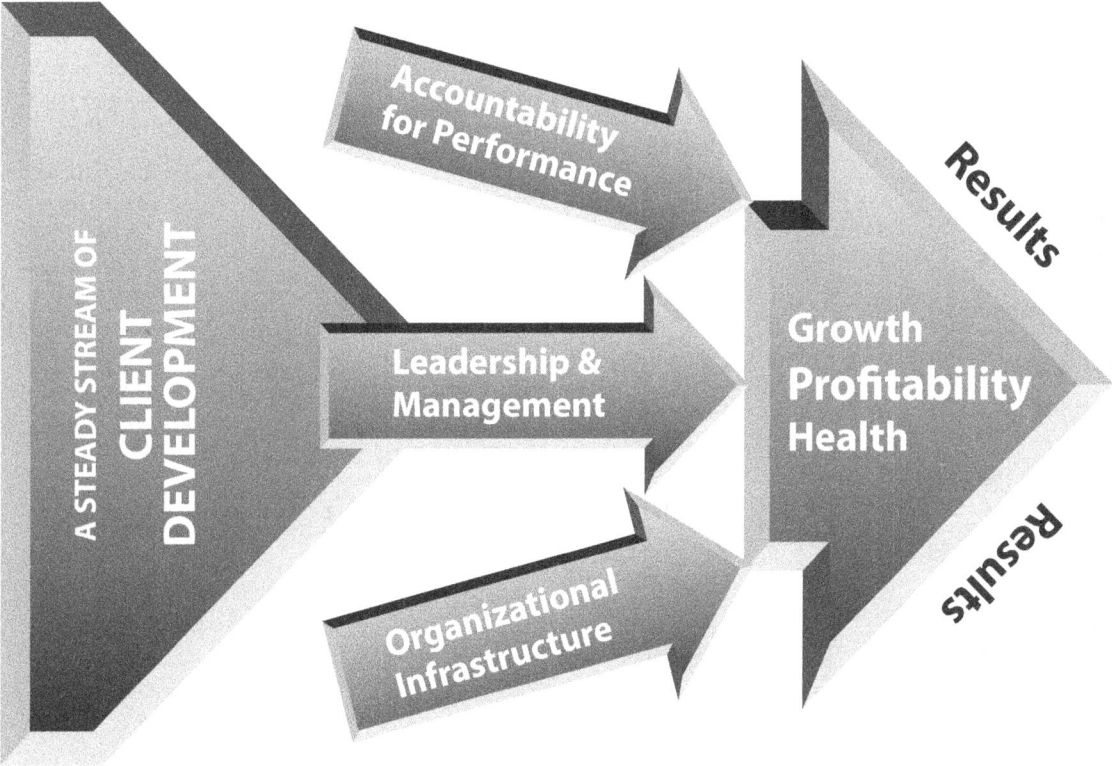

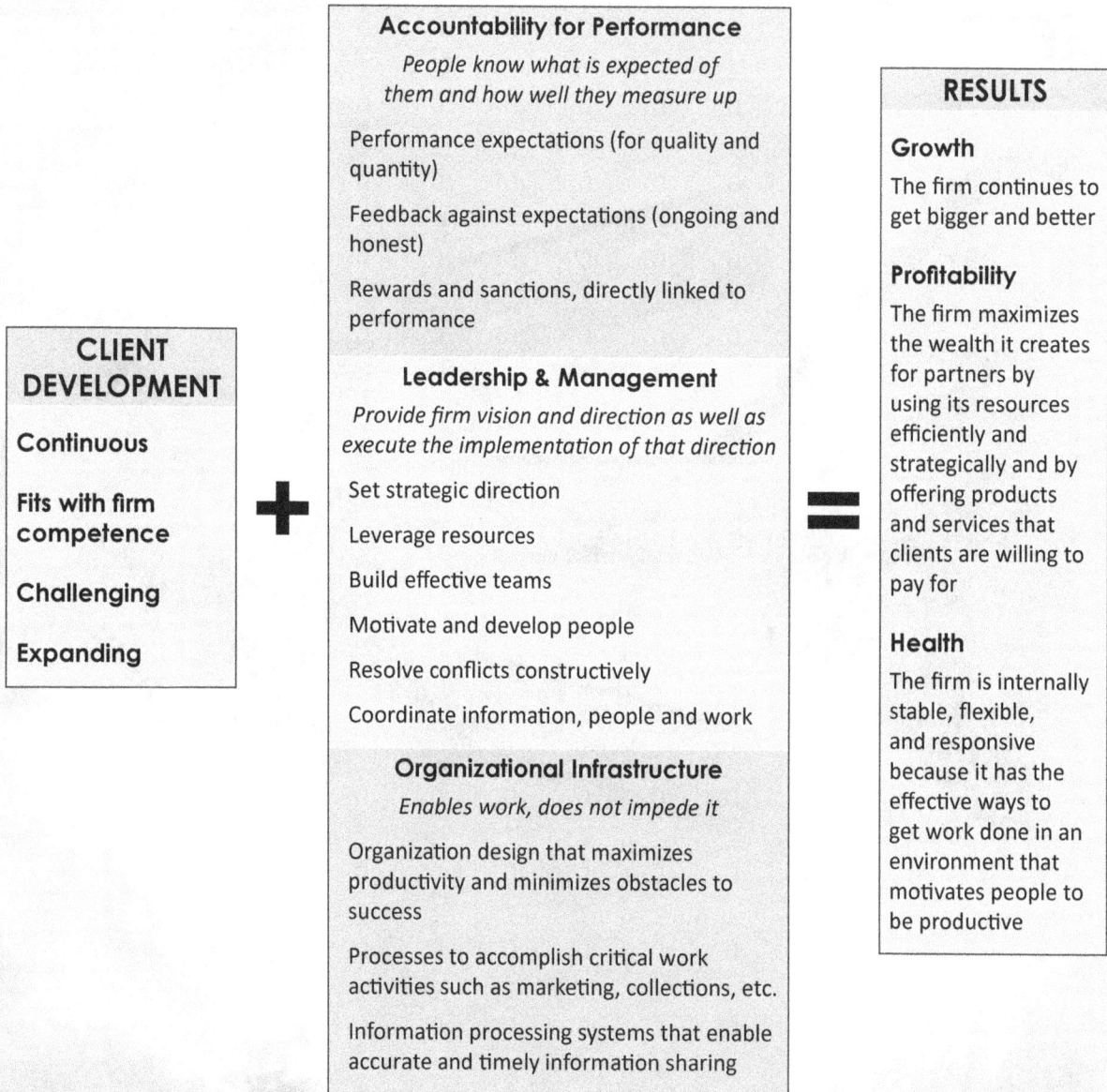

CLIENT DEVELOPMENT

Continuous

Fits with firm competence

Challenging

Expanding

+

Accountability for Performance

People know what is expected of them and how well they measure up

Performance expectations (for quality and quantity)

Feedback against expectations (ongoing and honest)

Rewards and sanctions, directly linked to performance

Leadership & Management

Provide firm vision and direction as well as execute the implementation of that direction

Set strategic direction

Leverage resources

Build effective teams

Motivate and develop people

Resolve conflicts constructively

Coordinate information, people and work

Organizational Infrastructure

Enables work, does not impede it

Organization design that maximizes productivity and minimizes obstacles to success

Processes to accomplish critical work activities such as marketing, collections, etc.

Information processing systems that enable accurate and timely information sharing

=

RESULTS

Growth

The firm continues to get bigger and better

Profitability

The firm maximizes the wealth it creates for partners by using its resources efficiently and strategically and by offering products and services that clients are willing to pay for

Health

The firm is internally stable, flexible, and responsive because it has the effective ways to get work done in an environment that motivates people to be productive

Post-Communicating Checklist

It is so important to do a post-consulting phase review to make sure that everything that needed doing was accomplished well and/or to identify areas that still need attention before moving forward in the consultation.

For each communicating topic below, rate yourself (3) well done; (2) needs more work; or (1) didn't do much and needs lots of attention. For items given a 1 or 2 rating, write down what you need to do prior to or during the next client meeting.

COMMUNICATING TOPIC	RATING	NEED TO DO
Data presentation created for maximum client impact		
Data-feedback meeting with client was effectively planned		
During data-feedback meeting, consultant(s) were able to adjust plan as needed		
Client was pleased and made progress toward self-mastery and project goal was a result of the feedback		
Feedback meeting content and process were tailored to the needs of the client		
Client was a co-equal contributor during the feedback meeting (consultants did not dominate)		
Feedback meeting with client led to an insightful diagnosis of the core issues related to the consulting challenge		
Client was satisfied with the deliverables		
Materials used in the meeting were well designed and professional		
Consultant(s) appeared professional and responsive to client		
If a consulting team, the team worked well together on behalf of the client		

CHAPTER 6
CHALLENGING | CONSULTING with THE ENNEAGRAM

There is nothing like a challenge to bring out the best in man [and women].
Sean Connery

Challenging a client to take the best action is a challenge in itself. Ideally, the client needs to be self-motivated to make any change, so how does a consultant help this to happen? Here you can read about how to do this, with a particular emphasis on Enneagram type-based defense mechanisms, ones that typically appear when major changes need to happen, as well as some tips about the best balance between confronting and supportive challenges for clients of each Enneagram type.

Challenging and the Enneagram

Post-challenging checklist

Challenging and the Enneagram

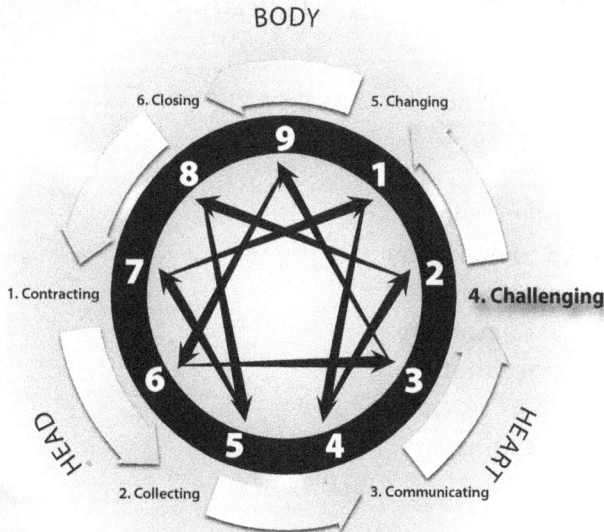

BODY

6. Closing

5. Changing

1. Contracting

4. Challenging

HEART

HEAD

2. Collecting

3. Communicating

CHALLENGING FOCUS AREAS

Do the client and consultant(s) both agree on the highest priority issues and root causes?

What is the optimal level of support versus confrontation needed by the client?

Is the client able, ready, and willing to take effective action?

How can the meeting be organized so the dialogue is extremely honest and respectful?

After the client has received the data feedback and prioritized the issues raised, the next step in the consulting process is the *Challenging* Stage – challenging the client to take action. While some clients may wish to proceed to the next to final stage, *Changing*, at this time, it is not recommended that the client launch directly into action planning.

There are several reasons not to skip the *Challenging* Stage. First, both clients and consultants need time to integrate the data collected and the conversations they have had during the *Communicating* Stage. New ideas, contrasting feelings, larger perspectives, and constructive questions usually emerge during this period; this "soak time" allows everything that has happened to sink in and settle. Many consultants allow their clients several days to consider the data before they meet again. This enables the clients to internalize the new information and do some serious self-reflection.

Second, the *Challenging* Stage is essential for motivating the client to change. Some clients will be ready to make changes after hearing the data from the data-feedback meeting, and some will not. Some may be willing to change, but be uncertain as to what the change will entail. In all cases, challenging the client requires him or her to take a hard look and ask: *Do I really want to change the organization in the ways required, and am I willing to change my own behavior?*

While challenging someone may not initially sound like a supportive type of behavior, when it is done with respect and compassion, it can become a turning point for many clients. In the consulting context, "challenging" refers to actions on the part of the consultant that startle the client and cause him or her to really take stock of organizational issues and his or her own behavior.

Types of Challenges

In coaching, there are essentially three types of challenges, as listed below. The first two are simple to do and fascinating to observe in action; the third challenge type is more complex, and it is extremely powerful.

The "What if....?" challenge

The "Why would you want to do that?" challenge

Paradox challenge

The "What if...?" Challenge

"What if" challenges work well in situations in which a client makes assumptions that something is important and inviolate. After hearing the client articulate an assumption, the coach poses a relevant "What if" question to the client.

The "Why would you want to do that?" Challenge

Asking this question of the client works effectively when clients say they want to change something about themselves. Clients may say they want to change something because they think it is a good idea; however, they may possess neither a deep desire to make the change nor the will and endurance required. Clients usually expect the coach to respond by saying, "That's great. How will you go about doing it?" not "Why would you want to do that?"

The Paradox Challenge

Paradoxes – apparent contradictions – pose frustrating yet motivating dilemmas for clients. The coaching client's paradox is this: The client truly wants something and believes that his or her behavior is designed to achieve that result. However, more often than not, the client's own behavior is the primary impediment to the achievement of his or her goals.

Enneagram Insights

When clients feel challenged to change – whether the consultant's challenge is supportive or assertive in tone, or emphasizes positive or negative information – the client's defense mechanisms become more active. Because of this, it is important to understand and recognize defensive patterns when they arise so that the consultant is prepared to not only help the client through the defensive response, but also to realize that when defenses are elicited, this is a moment of potential transformative work.

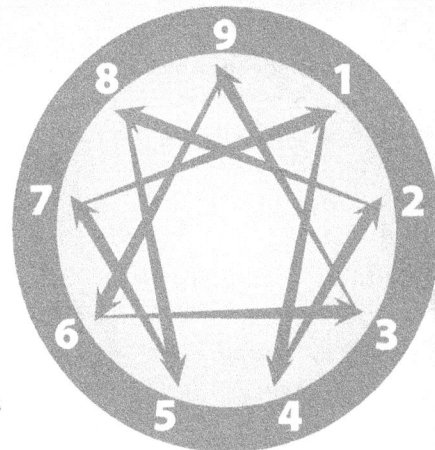

DEFENSE MECHANISMS

Everyone uses a variety of defense mechanisms when they feel anxious and in need of psychological protection, and even though people may be aware (or not) that they are feeling defensive, they are often unaware of what they are actually protecting at deeper levels. The Enneagram can be especially useful to consultants in recognizing the most important defense mechanisms of their clients because there is one defense mechanism in particular that individuals of each Enneagram style tend to use most often. This defensive structure is not only used repeatedly, it also appears when the clients feel the greatest unconscious need to armor themselves. This is the area that is actually the most important for their growth and forward movement. These are the most commonly used defense mechanisms for each Ennneagram style:

Ones | Reaction Formation

To control your impulses such as anger or other impulses you consider "bad" or potentially out of control, you keep your impulses outside your own awareness and do the opposite of your inclination.
Example: You dislike someone; instead, you are nice to him or her.
Additional defenses include repression, obsessive-compulsive behavior, and reactive anger.
Tip: Work with the client to acknowledge and understand the defensive reaction and to examine what is underneath it (hint: ask the client what he or she is really feeling) and/or frame the change as supporting improvement.

Twos | Repression

To keep your own needs under wraps (lest you be seen by yourself and others as needy), you keep your own needs and feelings (feelings are a clue to needs) out of your awareness and imagine other people need something from you.
Example: You need reassurance; instead, you give reassurance to the other person.
Additional defenses include interpersonal manipulation, martyrdom, and withdrawal.
Tip: Work with the client to acknowledge and understand the defensive reaction and to examine what is

underneath it (hint: ask the client what he or she needs *now*) and/or frame the change as supporting the intention to help others and help oneself.

Threes | Identification

To keep the idea that you are failing (or might fail) out of your awareness, you identify with whatever role you are playing or mask you are wearing, trying to convince yourself and others that you are the role or that the mask is real.

Example: You feel nervous before a big meeting; instead, your manner is completely poised and confident, never showing or expressing a trace of anxiety.

Additional defenses include emotional vacuum or confusion and over-activity.

Tip: Work with the client to acknowledge and understand the defensive reaction and to examine what is underneath it (hint: ask the client what he or she does when not working or what *being* as opposed to *doing* means) and/or frame the change as supporting goal achievement and success.

Fours | Introjection

To reinforce your feeling of deficiency, you take in (accept) as true other people's statements about or reactions to you because you lack sufficient filters to sort out what is true or not true, particularly with regard to negative data.

Example: Someone you know and like pays little attention to you at a social event; instead, you personalize this, assuming the person is mad at you or doesn't like you and then agonize over this for days.

Additional defenses include elitism, hyper-activity, depression (masking reservoirs of anger).

Tip: Work with the client to acknowledge and understand the defensive reaction and to examine what is underneath it (hint: Fours tend to introject negative information, but expel positive information). Focus on internalizing positive information and setting up better filters for negative information and/or frame the change as supporting the quest for excellence in self, others, and organizations.

Fives | Isolation

To avoid feeling overwhelmed and empty, you isolate yourself by going into your mind, cut yourself off from your feelings, and compartmentalize (isolate from one another) your thoughts, feelings, behaviors, and events in your life.

Example: Someone wants to discuss something important with you that has emotional content, but instead, you disconnect from both your feelings and your empathy for the other person by going into your intellect.

Additional defenses include obsessive strategizing.

Tip: Work with the client to acknowledge and understand the defensive reaction and to examine what is underneath it (hint: get the client to express feelings to you directly in the moment) and/or frame the change as supporting the acquisition of true knowledge through using information from the head, emotional realm, and learning from action.

Sixes | Projection

Instead of recognizing and acknowledging your own thoughts, feelings and behavior, you imagine that someone else is having these thoughts, feelings and reactions, although these are really projections of your own psyche onto the other person.

Example: Someone scares you, and because you want to do something to keep him or her from doing you harm, you imagine this person is out to get you.

Additional defenses include splitting others into all good and all bad and splitting self from others into good and bad.

Tip: Work with the client to acknowledge and understand the defensive reaction and to examine what is underneath it (hint: ask the client how he or she knows something to be true) and/or frame the change as creating more certainty and support through a systematic plan.

Sevens | Rationalization

To keep pain, discomfort, or worry that you might have done something wrong out of your awareness, you reframe the situation (give it a different context) so that your own behavior is justified, and you don't have to take responsibility for what has occurred.

Example: When you receive negative feedback, you create an explanation about why what you did had real value. For example, you say, "I was late to the meeting, but I created a new product on the way."

Additional defenses include idealization, devaluation, and blaming.

Tip: Work with the client to acknowledge and understand the defensive reaction and to examine what is underneath it (hint: reframe the rationalization) and/or re-frame the change as something that will be positive for them and others.

Eights | Denial

To prevent your weakness or vulnerability from coming into your awareness, you do not acknowledge – even to yourself – your personal, physical, and emotional limitations.

Example: You drive yourself to exhaustion, but do not become aware of it until you are ready to collapse.

Additional defenses include omnipotent control and extreme anger.

Tip: Work with the client to acknowledge and understand the defensive reaction and to examine what is underneath it (hint: ask the client to share his or her vulnerable feelings other than anger) and/or frame the change as creating more organizational movement and having things under control.

Nines | Narcotization

To avoid conflict and to create a comfortable harmonious feeling within you, you numb yourself by diffusing your attention and engaging in secondary activities such as gardening, chatting with other people, flipping television channels, cleaning house or taking a walk.

Example: You bring work home to do at night and instead, you clean the house and watch television.

Additional defenses include dissociation and passive-aggressive behavior.

Tip: Work with the client to acknowledge and understand the defensive reaction and to examine what is underneath it (hint: ask the client to give you clear opinions about something important to the work you are doing together) and/or frame the change as supporting harmony and cohesion.

BALANCING SUPPORT AND CONFRONTATION

When challenging clients, it is essential to find the right balance of support and confrontation. Support should never be collusive or coddling, but it should always be empathic and affirming. Confrontation should never be aggressive, but it should always be asserting and direct, even if gentle, kind and respectful. A very vulnerable client always needs more support than confrontation. A capable and confident client is better served with more confronting challenges than supportive ones. In addition, a client's Enneagram style can be very informative regarding how much support versus confrontation and when. Here are some guidelines:

Ones

Although some Ones can appear strong or even tough on the outside, many Ones really like warmth in their consultants and need to feel that the consultant believes in him or her and is not being judgmental (they are self-critical enough already). At the same time, Ones also need challenges that are confronting and not just supporting; this enables Ones to rise to the occasion, to not go into denial of the issues or their feelings, and to move beyond their comfort zone. And One clients will trust you more if you offer both support and confrontation.

Tip: Always be honest, whether it is supporting or confronting, because Ones sense dishonesty in others very quickly. If the situation facing the client is actually serious, then start with being simultaneously serious and supportive. For example, mention the gravity of the situation and how challenging it must be, then indicate some of the strengths the One client brings to the situation.

Twos

Twos actually appreciate some gentle confrontation, once they already feel support from the consultant, and this sense of support should have been established early on in the consulting relationship or it is already too late. Although Twos can feel very vulnerable, most Twos are not fragile and will take supportive confrontation as a sign of faith in them. Attuned empathy (meaning the empathic response is tuned into what the Two is actually feeling, even if he or she is not fully expressing it) is helpful, but only if followed by a call to action.

Tip: Be really careful to not try to flatter or in any way manipulate Twos into doing anything. Most Twos will resent being manipulated, so it isn't worth it and doing so will erode the trust they have in you.

Threes

Even though Threes are action oriented and don't appear to need much support, they actually need more gentle kindness than is apparent. Make sure to ask them how they are feeling, and if they seem to be in the throes of difficult emotions, hold off any confronting challenges until they have worked through what they feel.

Tip: Asking Threes what they really want is always an excellent question, although they may not have a ready answer to this. Give them time to consider their responses, and the more you wait, the more they learn. At the same time, if they really can't figure out the answer, offer them possible alternative answers. From this kind of prompt, many Threes can figure out whether your idea matches their response or what their own response truly is.

Fours

Fours usually want much more supportive challenges than confrontational ones, but...! Although highly supportive challenges may feel good to Fours, they don't always assist in the Four's forward movement. For example, if you commiserate with a Four client's predicament, this can help but only to a certain point; too much support can actually disable them from taking effective action, with the Four thinking, *Yes, even the consultant thinks this is an awful situation, so nothing can really be done about it!* However, if you try to get the Four to recognize the gravity of the situation by being too confronting, the Four client may simply become angry at the consultant instead of dealing with the real issues they face. This anger, then, becomes a convenient distraction for the client (even though their emotions feel real to them). And if the consultant affirms the Four client in a highly supportive way, the Four may become very distraught about receiving positive feedback because they are far more used to internalizing negative data about themselves. Oddly, support can feel like a confrontation to many Fours.

Tip: Recognize that what you intend may not be received the same way by the Four client, and don't take it personally. Instead, understand that this is part of their process. If you are patient, they will come around. And if there isn't really enough time for the Four client to take all the processing time he or she needs, bring this to his or her attention through a gentle confrontation, such as a story about how someone who took too long to resolve an issue missed out on something important.

Fives

Fives need challenges, both to their ways of thinking as well as to their experience and the identification of feelings. They also need challenges to take action that is different from what they would normally do. They need to get beyond their comfort zones. So does this mean a supportive challenge or a confronting challenge? When Fives are feeling vulnerable, support works best, as long as it is not patronizing in any way. When they are feeling less vulnerable but are just uncertain about how to do something, confronting challenges work better. For example, say, "You did this before; you can do it again!" is a confrontation to take action and not hide. This can help Fives gain confidence and move forward.

Tip: Pay close attention to the subtle shifts and changes in Five clients in order to calibrate their need for support and for more assertive challenges. When Five clients are more withdrawn, for example, they usually need more support, but be careful to not offer in a way that feels too emotional. When a Five client's skin is looking more alive (as if there is more blood flowing through it), they are usually ready for a slightly confronting challenge.

Sixes

Sixes want and need both support and confrontation, but the question for the consultant is when to do which and how to do it. If you know the Six client well and trust one another, the simplest way to determine the answer to this complicated question is to ask the client, "Which would be better now, some support or a strong challenge?" If you don't have a trusting relationship by this stage of the consultation, you need to work first with your client on how to improve your relationship!

Tip: The best tip is the one above: ask. However, here is one more: start with support, then move to gentle confrontation until you hit the level of confrontation the Six client can handle without becoming overly defensive. Sixes actually appreciate a smart confrontation, and they may even laugh when they hear it.

Sevens

Almost all Sevens really need support at first, so they feel empowered and safe enough (aka not-too-scared) to handle a confrontation, even a gentle one. The exception to this would be a highly aware Seven client who is in pain and in crisis. Then a clear, gentle confronting challenge can be invaluable.

Tip: It can be extremely useful to help Seven clients talk through other times when they have ably risen to face a similar difficult situation, asking for details and offering them specific, positive feedback about what you hear. As a result, Sevens get more in touch with the internal and external resources they actually possess, and this strengthens them to move forward.

Eights

Eights do like confronting challenges because they like challenges in general, but they also need more support than they even let themselves know. In general, start with a confronting challenge, but also offer support when they seem to need encouragement. Even a simple gesture of empathy feels like a great deal of support to most Eights.

Tip: Keep whatever you do simple, direct, useful, and smart. When Eight clients ask you what to do, tell them exactly what you think, and be honest. Even if you say, "I want you to tell me what you want to do or why you are perplexed and then I'll tell you," Eight clients will appreciate your straightforwardness.

Nines

Most Nines strongly prefer supportive challenges, and they like their confronting challenges to be done in a gentle and non-directive way. However, at times, Nines really do need more confrontation to get them out of their routines and comfort zones. Although Nines like routine and predictability, it is also essential to tap into their excitement and drive for something new when you issue a more confronting challenge. For example, you can say, "If things keep going as they currently are, you're going to get exactly what you have. Is that what you want?"

Tip: Ask their permission to issue a more confronting challenge. This will arouse their curiosity. They may say, "Maybe later," but they may also say, "OK!"

Post-Challenging Checklist

It is so important to do a post-consulting phase review to make sure that everything that needed doing was accomplished well and/or to identify areas that still need attention before moving forward in the consultation.

For each challenging topic below, rate yourself (3) well done; (2) needs more work; or (1) didn't do much and needs lots of attention. For items given a 1 or 2 rating, write down what you need to do prior to or during the next client meeting.

CHALLENGING TOPIC	RATING	NEED TO DO
Client issues were prioritized accurately		
Offered the optimal level of support versus challenge		
Client understands the issues and their root causes		
Client is motivated and ready to take effective action		
Client felt treated with dignity and respect		
Client was able to raise concerns and vulnerabilities		
Consultant(s) was responsive to client needs and feelings		
New insights occurred for the client, consultant(s), or both		
The team worked well together on behalf of the client (if a consulting team was involved)		

CHAPTER 7
CHANGING | CONSULTING with THE ENNEAGRAM

If you want truly to understand something, try to change it.
Kurt Lewin

Changing organizations, cultures, teams, and individuals is a complex task that takes time, skill, and continuous readjustments in real time. No matter how well planned and orchestrated the change, something is called to your attention that says, "Even though this should have worked well or it did the last time we tried it, it isn't now!" Hopefully, if the prior 6-C Consulting Stages have gone well, the Changing Stage is set up for success. The following materials will help during the Changing Stage:

Intervention (change) technologies

OD interventions

Organizational change model | transitions

Change strategy formula

The best of organizational change

Best practices benchmark report

Post-changing checklist

Changing and the Enneagram

BODY

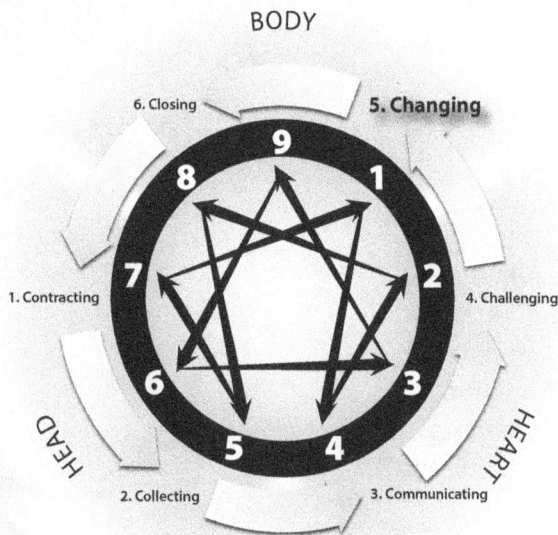

CHANGING FOCUS AREAS

What does the client really want to change?

Why does the client want to change and is this enough?

How will the client know when the change has occurred (including outcome measures)?

Does the client have both a viable plan for and a way to support and sustain the change?

Are there any other areas that need attention, as yet un-discussed or unresolved?

Does the client (and the organization) "own" the change or are they dependent on the consultant(s)?

By the time the consulting relationship reaches the final stage, *Changing*, the client has more often than not already begun the process of change – *if* the following criteria have been met:

The contracting was clear, complete, and renegotiated as needed.

The data-collection process asked the right people the right questions.

The data was effectively communicated, was organized to suit the client's goals and learning style, and included an honest dialogue between the consultant and client.

The client felt constructively challenged by the consultant.

The success of the *Changing* Stage is dependent on the success of the first four stages, with errors or omissions during the first four causing a variety of problems during the *Changing* Stage. For example, if the contracting was unclear, the client may begin to shuttle between several alternative goals for change, losing focus and, frequently, the commitment to the consulting process. Also, if the data that has been collected is either incomplete or inconclusive, clients typically respond by being less willing to take action later on, as they are likely unsure of what to do or how to do it. When data is not effectively communicated because of the way in which it has been organized or presented, clients can lose interest in the consulting process. Finally, if there is no challenge to clients, they are far less motivated to take action or to follow-up on action they have agreed to take.

The majority of clients, however, will have already begun to change to some degree. Some may have begun to show improvement during the *Collecting* Stage: they may already have been aware of the behaviors they needed to work on and so had begun to work on these in anticipation of the expected data. Change may also occur during the *Communicating* Stage, particularly if the data includes concrete suggestions for improvement. For example, the feedback may include a statement such as, "The leader needs to hold staff meetings on a regular basis and not cancel scheduled meetings," or "The organization is siloed, with each part functioning separate from the other." Clients may immediately discuss this issue with the consultant to determine a solution and begin implementation immediately.

Of change that occurs prior to the actual *Changing* Stage, the most profound often takes place after the consultant has challenged the client. The client's and/or client system's self-reflection moves to a deeper level; as awareness increases, clients understand their old behaviors in new ways, frequently begin to identify their underlying motivations, repetitive thinking patterns, and deeper feelings, and begin changing the way they address issues and shape the organization.

During the final stage, *Changing*, the consultant's job is to help clients focus their efforts through the accomplishment of the following tasks:

Reconfirming goals and outcomes

Defining criteria for success – that is, how the client will know that the goals have been reached

Developing a plan

Identifying resources the client will need to support sustained change

Reconfirming goals

Here, the consultant can ask the client: "Considering all that you have learned, what do you really want to change?" When the client's goals remain unchanged from those identified during the *Contracting* Stage, the consulting conversation can move to the next step – defining success criteria. However, when the client has new or additional goals, it is helpful to compare these to the initial goals and to readjust as needed.

Reconfirming outcome measures

How will the client know when a goal has been reached? Most people assume that success criteria are so obvious that no discussion is necessary. Here is a good place to discuss the four Balanced Scorecard areas and to define the desired outcomes in each area:

Financial Perspective

Customer Perspective

Internal Business Process Perspective

Learning and Growth Perspective

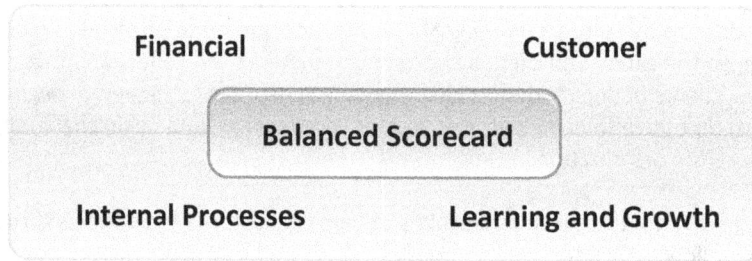

Financial	Customer
Balanced Scorecard	
Internal Processes	Learning and Growth

Enneagram Insights

HEAD CENTER | TRUST AND FAITH

Trust between the consultant and client is usually on the mind of Head Center clients throughout all phases of the consulting project. Thus, they have already observed the client in action and have likely drawn conclusions about whether or not the consultant is trustworthy. In a sense, clients have to feel safe enough with the consultant to take the further risks that changing themselves and the organization entails.

The client must trust that the consultant:

Will continue to maintain confidentiality

Will not usurp the leader's authority or position in the organization

Has the knowledge and skills to assist the client through the next stages of the project

The client must also have trust in the organization – for example, that there is no ulterior motive behind the consulting, such as an impending demotion, or that anyone in the organization will pressure the consultant to reveal information or to alter the consulting contract. Going into the action phase of the consulting project will involve many unknowns, ambiguity, and uncertainty, all of which may last months or even years. For these reasons, clients will need to take a leap of faith with the project and the work of the consultant. The implementation plans – which decrease uncertainty and increase predictability – will be exceedingly important to Fives, Sixes, and Sevens. While these issues will be of concern to anyone who agrees to use a consultant, they will be more worrisome for individuals with head-based Enneagram styles (Five, Six, and Seven).

HEART CENTER | IMAGE AND PRIDE

As the consulting project proceeds to the action stage, it becomes increasingly public. Because of this, the three Enneagram styles based in the Heart Center will become increasingly concerned about both how the project will be perceived by others and how they will be perceived by others. If they appear as "failed leaders," because either the project does not go well or they appear too dependent on the consultant, Twos, Threes, and Fours will experience a blow to their professional image and stature. In this sense, any lack of success or the perception that they are in any way inadequate will puncture their pride. Helping them do the following can be very helpful: (1) facilitating an impact analysis for the change, (2) developing an effective communication strategy for the project, and (3) assisting them with a public relations effort related to the project and their careers. While everyone using a consultant will have the above issues on their minds, the heart-based styles (Two, Three, and Four) will tend to be most concerned about them because of their preoccupation with image and interpersonal acceptance.

BODY CENTER | CONTROL AND OUTCOMES

Issues of control will appear throughout all phases of the consultation, but this is particularly the case at the stage of taking action. The key questions include: *What actions will be taken, who will take these actions, and who will make these decisions?* These questions go beyond the client and consultant; they also include the client system, others who will be impacted by the decisions, authority figures in organizational hierarchy, and others. It is extremely important to body-based clients that they feel in control of decisions, processes used, and outcomes, and it is the job of the consultant to help the client feel in control and, at the same time, fully partnered with the consultant in decisions, processes, and outcomes. It is also critical for the consultant to help the client consider when and why to involve others in the process.

Eights may tend to move too quickly to action without all the necessary pieces of the project being in place, and may not have included necessary others in their thought processes or decision-making. This can create unnecessary resistance to the change. Nines may move slowly or become inert or angry if they feel overwhelmed by the magnitude of the changes needed or if they feel forced to do something. They may also tend to make many decisions by consensus when they should be making the decisions themselves, using the consultant as a sounding board. Ones may focus on details of the change at the expense of the big picture or they may try to take on too much work at the implementation stage without delegating work to others or building the teams required to implement the work.

Although individuals of all styles carry these concerns, they tend to be forefront in the minds of the three body-based styles (One, Eight, and Nine) for whom issues of control are central to the personality structure.

Intervention (Change) Technologies

Change can occur when directed at one or multiple targets. Targeted change interventions aimed at the targets closest to the root causes generate the most change, and multiple targets aimed in the same direction create even more change. The choice of change technology is equally important to effect the desired change, with some technologies better suited for certain kinds of change. Here are many options:

INTERVENTION (CHANGE) TARGET	INTERVENTION (CHANGE) TECHNOLOGY
Individual	Coaching | Other diagnostics | 360^0 feedback | Career planning | Leadership development Motivation | Role clarification | Emotional intelligence
Pair	Conflict resolution | Role clarification | Communication | Feedback
Team	Role clarification | Conflict resolution | Group process | Team development Work redesign | Social networks | Communication | Tavistock | Process consultation Problem solving | Goal setting | Change management
Business unit	Organization redesign | Visioning | Strategic planning | Process re-engineering Culture change | Reward systems | Problem solving | Change management
Inter-group or inter-business unit	Conflict resolution | Role clarification | Collaboration
Organization | total system	TQM (total quality management) | Visioning | Strategic planning | Organization redesign Culture change | Diversity | Whole systems change conferences | Reward systems Process re-engineering | Succession planning | Performance management Talent management | Balanced scorecard
Process technologies Useful with units ranging from teams to inter-organizational and communities or inter-community work	Action research | Future search | Open systems | Appreciative inquiry | Systems thinking

OD Interventions or "Help! What Do I Do Now?"
By Ginger Lapid-Bogda, PhD

© Ginger Lapid- Bogda, Ph.D., "OD Interventions or Help! What Do I Do Now?" in *Organization Development and Consulting: Perspectives and Foundations*, Fred Massarik and Marissa Pei-Carpenter, eds. Jossey-Bass/Pfeiffer, 2002.

The most complex display of the variety of interventions used by organization development consultants can be found in Blake and Mouton's (1983) "Consulcube" from their book *Consultation*. This three-dimensional cube looks at who the client is (called "units of change"), the consultation style used ("kinds of interventions"), and problem(s) diagnosed ("focal issues"). See the layout below.

Units of Change | individual | group | intergroup | organization | larger social system

Kind of Interventions | acceptant | catalytic | confrontation | prescriptive | theory and principles

Focal Issues | power and authority | morale and cohesion | norms and standards | goals and objectives

Schmuck and Mile (1976), in *OD in Schools*, construct an intervention cube that adds dyad/triad to the "Units of Change" dimension and role to "Focal Issues." The Schmuck and Miles Intervention Dimension includes consultant style and the process used by the consultant (that is, data feedback, process consultation, task force establishment, and so forth). W. Warner Burke (1982) provides a readable narrative of these and other intervention typologies in *Organization Development: Principles & Practices*. But do OD consultants actually use cubes in making determinations about how to intervene in client systems? We might use one, after the fact, to describe what we've done. We might also use a cube before an intervention to assess our options. However, the remaining sections of this paper depict more of what we actually *do* using analysis and intuition. They are, I think, the mind and guts of our work.

Organization Diagnosis

Consultants have models, categories, and working theories (implicit and explicit) about how organizations work, how people behave, and how change occurs. These help us and our clients make sense out of an otherwise chaotic world; without them we wouldn't know what questions to ask, how to organize data, or how to engage in dialogue with a client about organization problems or growth. These models also limit us as we leave elements out of our models. At one time I added strategy and positioning to my conceptual framework and later I added vision and the importance of leadership in setting vision and strategic direction. Now that I look at these issues, I actually see them and work with them in most of my consultations. In sum, we intervene where we see weaknesses and strengths, but what we see is determined by the models we use.

Hurting Systems

The organization diagnosis would tell us which part of the organization is in the most pain and, therefore, the most potentially motivated to work on change. The mottos "no pain, no gain" and "when you ain't got nothing, you got nothing to lose" apply here. One client came to me with a "presenting problem" of lack of teamwork. The diagnosis stage indicated an all-out racial war. The issue behind this was a leadership vacuum of ten years. But the obvious pain was in the racial conflicts, which is where the client members were first willing to do the work.

Success Interventions

The client and client system may need to experience something successful together before they are willing to work on deeper, more powerful issues. Or the client may need to have a success with the consultant before the client will use the consultant on a more complex or more expensive problem. I came upon this latter aspect with a client who wanted to use me in an action research project *after* they had seen me do something. They, however, could think of nothing for me to do with them – I was supposed to come to a meeting with them and do something! After I got past my resentment at "being on stage" and my nervousness ("stage fright"), I worked with them to explore how the position they put me in reflected some of their own issues and then discussed what they hoped might result from our working together. I got the contract.

Domino Analysis

I first heard this term from Dick Beckhard in a presentation. As a problem area surfaces, it requires us to ask, "What is the cause of the problem?" and then to ask the question again and again until you get to the root problem. Once at the core, the intervention can begin. A large-scale contract presented our consulting team with a "presenting problem" or morale. This was, however, a symptom of departmental chaos: every department lacked coherent structure, policies, and communication systems. Behind this was the core issue of managerial competence and leadership. The managers were all very inexperienced and they felt neglected, at best, and victimized, at worst, by the parent organization. So we began our intervention through intensive management coaching and, during the group feedback segment of the action research project, the managers facilitated the meetings with the OD consultant in the role of coach and backup support. This was done to enable the managers to be proactive at each step.

Backup Method

While this sounds like the domino analysis, it is quiet different. In the "backup method", the consultant is the stage director. Here, the consultant asks, "If this intervention is to be successful, what other elements must be in place?" These elements are not core problems; they simply help things along. A recent contract for a three-day retreat with a management team of thirty people focused on direction and purpose for an entire organization. "Backing up", my co-consultant and I met with the leadership pair for a consultation to explore their individual and common values and visions in preparation for their presentation at the retreat. We also requested that the managers do some preparation regarding their visions and values for their departments. These "backup" interventions allowed the retreat experience to become more thorough, reflective, and mutual.

Historical Successes and Failures

In determining an appropriate intervention for an organization with a particular problem, an assessment of the organization's history of OD successes and failures can tell the consultant what might and might not work with the client. It can tell you what may be the effect of a certain process, as well as what type of "halo effect" an intervention may have, simply because it is similar in method to a prior positive or negative intervention process.

As an example, a human resource group with whom I consult requested a team-building retreat. The obvious question was why they wanted it. The answer given was that they felt they needed it. As I explored with them why their prior experience has been negative, two themes emerged: the agenda had been the manager's, not the group's, and the consultant had colluded with the department in not facing highly conflicting issues. As a result of this information (and so as not to encourage a negative "halo effect"), the intervention design was as follows: (1) generate the issues needing attention by having each group member anonymously complete two 3" x 5" cards – the first card answered the question, "What two or three issues do we need to deal with that would be easy for us?" and the second card responded to the question, "What two or three areas do we need to address as a group that are difficult for us to deal with but which would add great value to our organization if we could deal with them effectively?;" (2) collect the cards and read them out loud; (3) divide the group into small groups of three or four people and have each group design the next two days; (4) compare and combine designs according to group consensus; (5) negotiate the consultant role regarding confrontational consultant behavior (which they preferred to call "gutsy"); and (6) do it.

Consultant Strength and Stretch

At the negative extreme of consultant strength would be the consultant who is so specialized that every consultation intervention, no matter what the client needs, is, for example, "quality circles," "team building," or "work redesign." At the extreme of consultant stretch is the consultant who has been wanting to try an intervention so that the next client, regardless of the organizational issues, receives that intervention. The extremes aside, most competent consultants do factor strength and stretch into their practices. My own example feels like true confessions of a consultant. I am quite adept at group process (strength) and have a limited attention span (forty-five-minute intervals at best) for facilitating task-only problem solving meetings (weakness). Consequently, if the client needs task-specific group problem solving, I often break participants into small groups where they facilitate themselves, or I coach the head of the group in task-specific meeting leadership and then support the leader through process consultation and make task-related interventions only when the group gets "stuck." My true confession relates to stretch: with any client I always look for some way(s) to do something new. I look for what is unique about the client and the client's issues to assess how I can be creative and stimulated. This approach, I think, keeps me vital and authentic as a consultant and person. The above items are beginning explorations of what I think real consultants do. They do *not* use "cubes" or any other mechanistic categorization of interventions as a priori categories. They develop congruent approaches from experience, leading, talking with colleagues, and self-reflection.

In doing the self-reflection, I realized that I believe an intervention actually starts when the client make the decision to act by calling the consultant. Consequently, the intervention stage doesn't occur after diagnosis, but starts with the initial call. Peter Block (2000) explores these early interventions in *Flawless Consulting*, particularly those related to contracting and resistance. In all this our own styles as unique human beings are basic.

time for change

Organizational Change Model | Transitions

This organizational change model, developed by Dick Beckhard in the 1970s, has withstood the test of time. Almost every contemporary model of change is based on this easy-to-understand – but harder to do – concept. In order for change to occur, you must articulate the desired future state; assess the current organizational situation in relation to the preferred future; then design an effective transition process to get from where you are to where you want to be. In addition, the current business still needs attention and must be well run, and this must be done throughout the change process.

FUTURE STATE

TRANSITION

Business as usual...

PRESENT STATE

Change Strategy Formula

$$D \times V \times P > R = C$$

This change formula is a strategy for implementing change and can be used prior to a change effort, at milestone intervals during a change, or at the end of a change as a retrospective debriefing. The basic concept is this: to get change (C), you have to have sufficient demand, desire or dissatisfaction with the current situation (D), a compelling, shared vision for getting to a preferred future (V), a viable plan to achieve this vision (P), and all three factors must be greater than the resistance to the change (R) for the change to occur. In addition, (1) the greater the D, V and P, the greater the change, and (2) if any of these three factors (D, V, or P) is 0, there will be no change at all.

D = increase the demand and desire for change

Educate people on the need for change

Paint best-case and worst-case scenarios

Get employees and managers to collect data themselves

Refrain from insulating people from the problem

Conduct focus groups and interviews to get people talking about the issues

Bring in outside statistics

Use external experts to make the case

Do benchmarking

V = the vision or model of change

Develop a collaborative vision

Communicate the vision with passion (stories, metaphors, real people)

Communicate continuously using multiple media

Articulate compelling values

Use organizational models and frameworks to paint the case

Enlist top management as spokespersons

Use benchmarking results

P = the plan or process for the change

Develop a relevant, flexible planning process

Use effective change models to develop the plan

Communicate the planning process (make it transparent)

Involve relevant groups (internal and external) in the planning process

Use interdisciplinary task forces and ad hoc advisory groups

Make certain the planning group has the time, resources, stature, and expertise to lend credibility to the process

Conduct impact analyses and work this information into the plan

Develop a master plan as well as sub-plans (e.g., communications, financial, logistics, buy-in, etc.)

R = resistance to the change

Identify the sources of resistance and develop strategies to respond

Set up transparent formal and informal participation structures

Clarify where input is helpful and where input can't be utilized (state the givens)

Listen to feedback; take action when appropriate

Demonstrate publicly how and when input is being used

Help people deal with attachment and loss (allow time, opportunities for expressing emotions, ceremonies and rituals for letting go and starting new)

Help people understand that resistance is a natural part of change

Reward effective behavior in the direction of the change through formal and informal rewards, thinking in terms of both financial rewards, but also non-financial or symbolic rewards

Know what the resistance is on an on-going basis, use it in constructive ways, and don't over-focus on it

The Best of Organizational Change

Why do many organizational change efforts fail, while others succeed? The answers are in this condensed version of the change practices – taken from the work of John Kotter, 6 Sigma, David Nadler, and other sources – that create the best and most long-lasting change results.

LEADERS MUST LEAD THE CHANGE	Without this, the change will not occur; coalitions must be utilized in addition to individual champions; leadership must be visible, congruent, and credible
Generate a Shared Sense of Urgency	A desire for change needs to be continuously communicated so that complacency does not set in; highlighting problems or defects is one way; in addition, potential opportunities create a positive approach
Create and Communicate a Compelling Vision	The vision must be shared, based on both environmental scanning and organization values; strive for world-class; the vision must be repeated and communicated continuously through multiple media
Design and Convey Strategies for Achieving the Vision	The strategies must be high level, and comprehensive enough to accomplish the vision; they must also be flexible
Develop a Comprehensive Implementation Plan	Develop a systematic implementation plan that covers all aspects of the change and includes a thorough impact analysis, a communication plan, a logistics plan, timetables, key milestones, and accountabilities
Mobilize Commitment and Empower Employees for Action	Commitment must be engendered from key people and groups and widespread support must be developed; people need to be empowered and trained with regards to the direction of the change; rewards and sanctions should include actions related to the desired change
Make Lasting Change, Both Short Term Wins and Long Term, Systemic Transformation	Visible short term change precedes strategic long term change; strategic long term change must be root cause-based and deal with systemic issues; it should focus on changing systems and structures
Monitor Progress	Progress must be monitored at regular intervals and include agreed upon measures; in addition, progress should be assessed at unpredictable times as a hedge against surface compliance
Consolidate Gains and Redouble Efforts	The change effort should be reassessed, adjustments made, and strategies developed for energizing the initiative; this should happen on a periodic basis, both planned and as needed
Anchor the Changes in the New Organization	The changes need to be institutionalized in the new organization or the organization can revert back to its prior patterns; develop rituals, rewards and generate enthusiasm through continuous communication

BEST PRACTICES ENNEAGRAM IN BUSINESS

BENCHMARK REPORT

ARGENTINA

AUSTRALIA

BOLIVIA

BRAZIL

CANADA

CHILE

CHINA

COLOMBIA

CZECH REPUBLIC

DENMARK   FINLAND

URUGUAY

UNITED STATES

THAILAND

SOUTH AFRICA

JAPAN

ITALY

IRAN

GERMANY

FRANCE

Adcock Ingram   Avon   Banco Itaú   Banco Nossa Caixa   Beacon   Best Buy   Culture Technology

Daimler/Mitsubishi   Genentech/Roche   Hanfubuki   Hui Ho'olana   Huron Hospital   La Clinica   Milling Hotels

NuEar   Parker Hinneafen   Shahid Ghandi   StarPoint   Sucromiles   Toyota   Veloso Consultores   and more

Benchmark Team

Matt Ahrens (US) | Lindy Amos (Australia) | Valerie Atkin (US) | Gema de la Rosa (Spain)
Neil Harper (South Africa) | Martin Hawkes (Ireland) | Gloria Hung (China)
Ginger Lapid-Bogda (US) | Bo Zoffman (Denmark)

A special report of The Enneagram in Business Network (EIBN)

JULY 2011

Overview: best practices benchmark study
lessons learned from 72 companies
a 2011 benchmark study conducted by The Enneagram in Business Network

Although thousands of organizations worldwide use the Enneagram in a variety of business applications, 72 companies have been using the Enneagram intensively to dramatically develop their leaders and teams; enhance emotional intelligence and interpersonal competence among their employees; and catalyze culture change.

Background: What can we learn from these trailblazers? We conducted 39 in-depth interviews with leaders and consultants from all over the world – all with track records of success using the Enneagram in organizations – to give us the answers. We talked with consultants and leaders from more than 20 countries spanning 5 continents: Argentina, Australia, Bolivia, Brazil, Canada, Chile, China, Colombia, Czech Republic, Denmark, Finland, France, Germany, Iran, Italy, Japan, South Africa, Thailand, United States, and Uruguay.

The consultants and leaders included members of the Enneagram in Business Network (EIBN) as well as non-members. All interviewees had used the Enneagram a minimum of 18 months in their organizations, with some as long as 12 years.

Companies: All interviews were conducted with the promise of anonymity; however, 21 companies gave us permission to use their names: Adcock Ingram, Avon, Banco Itaú, Banco Nossa Caixa, Beacon, Best Buy, Culture Technology, Daimler/Mitsubishi, Genentech/Roche, Hanfubuki, Hui Ho'olana, Huron Hospital, La Clinica, Milling Hotels, NuEar, Parker Hinneafen, Shahid Ghandi, StarPoint, Sucromiles, Toyota, and Veloso Consultores.

Industries: Companies in this study represent the following industries: biotech, chemical, education, finance, government, health care, hospitality, insurance, IT, manufacturing, non-profits, petroleum, pharmaceutical, professional associations, research, retail, service, and transportation.

Key Question: We were interested in the answer to this question: *What success have organizations experienced using the Enneagram in their companies; how did they achieve this; and what lessons were learned along the way?* We thought it was time to offer a comprehensive answer!

Results: The results summarized on the following pages will, we believe, make an important contribution to leaders, human resource professionals, and consultants in creating productive, sustainable, and conscious organizations.

Best practices: critical success factors

the top 6 factors (in rank order) | what 39 experts say is critical to the success of a productive and sustainable enneagram-based organizational change

Introduction

Of the 39 experts interviewed, 6 critical success factors emerged as essential to a successful, sustainable Enneagram-based organizational change. Whether the interviewees were leaders or consultants and regardless of their industry, country, or company size, their answers were strikingly similar.

Success Factor 1 | Focus on real needs: business *and* personal (82%)

According to the experts, the single most important critical success factor for an effective Enneagram-based change effort is that it focus on the organization's real needs, as well as the specific needs of leaders, teams, and employees. The business needs varied – interactions, leadership, sales, engagement, performance management, EQ, conflict, culture change, productivity, moving from a local to a global marketplace, as examples – but the message was the same: set clear, realistic, and important goals that really matter to the organization and achieve demonstrable results. But, just as important was the direct personal benefit in their lives outside of work.

"There is a huge unmet need at work and at home. At work, the need involves creativity, empathy, and flexibility and being less hierarchical and more networked. At home, there's more stress, huge demands, and increasing complexity. The Enneagram helps with all of this."

Success Factor 2 | Strong leadership: organizational commitment (69%)

Support from the top leaders provides credibility, authority, visible support, resources for a sustainable change, and personal testimonials that convince others of the value of the Enneagram. In addition, it is important to enlist support and commitment from middle managers, who provide the impetus for effective execution.

"Leaders have to deeply desire development for themselves and for others."

Success Factor 3 | Enneagram typing: balanced, accurate self-discovery (66%)

The most effective way to determine one's type is guided self-discovery, because it is the most accurate, engaging, and insightful approach. Just as important, a context must be set by consultants, leaders, and organizations that avoids stereotypes and psychological or esoteric jargon, focuses on development and potential, and embraces a respect for differences.

"Avoid labeling; go beyond the numbers to integration."

Success Factor 4 | Highest quality: consultants, workshops, and change interventions (56%)

Quality is essential in the facilitator or consultant chosen, the workshops offered, and the change activities that are implemented. Consultants must be knowledgeable about both the Enneagram and organizational change processes; provide stimulating, interactive workshops; present information in a non-judgmental, insightful, and accurate way; and encourage participation, being responsive to all concerns and questions.

Workshops, programs, and interventions must be innovative, adapted to the needs and culture of the organization, and conducted in a learning environment of safety, excitement, and fun.

"The consultant's depth of experience and expertise is essential to the credibility of the Enneagram and the linkage to organizational needs."

Success Factor 5 | Fully integrated within organization (54%)

The Enneagram must be used long enough in a targeted array of applications so it becomes part of everyday worklife; this provides real-time practice and promotes a higher transfer of learning. In addition, ongoing, stimulating opportunities need to be offered that employ multiple learning modalities: for example, 1-1 development meetings; ongoing workshops; eLearning; websites; smartphone Apps; books; informal discussions; team interactions, and innovative pilot programs.

"A hybrid of interventions within a continuous, coordinated, and flexible plan."

Success Factor 6 | Cultural readiness (33%)

To be receptive to the power of the Enneagram, organizations need to have sufficient trust, openness, curiosity, respect, and willingness to try something new.

"Without sufficient readiness, employees would fear the Enneagram could be used as a weapon."

CRITICAL SUCCESS FACTORS FROM 39 EXPERTS

82% of the experts agreed that focus on real needs was the single most important critical success factor.

There was also strong agreement about the next four factors: leadership, typing, quality, and integration. This was consistent in every industry, every country, and whether the interviewee was a consultant or a leader.

The final factor, cultural readiness, while important, was not as critical as the other five factors.

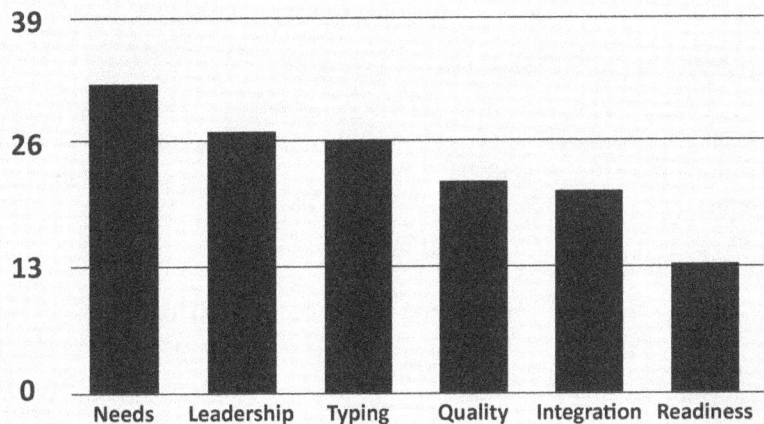

Applications of the enneagram
what the best companies actually do

Introduction

Over 25 Enneagram-business applications were mentioned by interviewees; here are the top 10.

Application 1 | Communication

Communication applications include the following: increased understanding of differences in communication style; minimizing Enneagram-based communication distortions and misperceptions; and enhancing interactions between people of the 9 types. These are done through ongoing programs, workshops, Enneagram type panels, and 1-1 coaching.

Application 2 | Leadership

Leadership development applications include organization-wide leadership development programs; competency-based leadership learning communities; individual coaching; and development programs for target groups – i.e., high potentials and women. Many of these monthly, weeklong, or series of one-day workshops are designed for specific needs: to create greater leadership bench strength; to instill a culture of development; and to reduce reliance of hierarchy, competition and control, while increasing collaboration and innovation.

Application 3 | Teams

These teams include executive level, management teams, and intact work teams that meet in-person, virtually, or a combination of both. The focus includes enhancing team behavior at the individual and team level (including team dynamics); creating high-performing and self-organizing teams; eliminating team dysfunction; and team mergers. Programs vary from day-long sessions to 1+ years.

Application 4 | EQ | Personal Development

Referred to as Emotional Intelligence (EQ), self-mastery, and personal development, these applications are initiated to increase *intra-* and *inter*-personal competence. These efforts (via workshops and coaching) increase self-understanding, self-acceptance and self-management, but also enhance compassion and improve interactions.

Application 5 | Coaching

In-person or by phone, formally and informally, Enneagram coaching is being used for talent and performance management, leadership development, EQ, and more. In addition, some companies train managers to coach their employees using the Enneagram.

Application 6 | Conflict

Whether in family businesses, law firms, corporations, or non-profits and governments, using the Enneagram to reduce conflict depersonalizes the issues, making them far easier to resolve. This application occurs between the conflicting parties, as stand-alone training programs, or within teams.

Application 7 | Feedback

This application is usually combined with other training topics (i.e., communication, conflict, leadership) or taught by itself to employees as well as leaders.

Application 8 | Decision Making

Because this application enables people to reduce their type based decision-making biases, it occurs most often in leadership and team development programs.

Application 9 & 10 | Sales and Negotiations

Both applications involve increasing one's capabilities (sales or negotiation) through self-development and also by adjusting one's approach to the type of the other person.

APPLICATION AREA	Companies using this application
1. Communication	49/72
2. Leadership	44/72
3. Teams	41/72
4. EQ	36/72
5. Coaching	35/72
6. Conflict	33/72
7. Feedback	31/72
8. Decision Making	18/72
9. Sales	13/72
10. Negotiations	12/72

The data showed that while no single enneagram-business application is being used by every company, most organizations are using at least 4-5, with some using as many as 13.

Surprises!
what we didn't know for sure, but do now

Surprise 1 | PROFOUND RESULTS

Companies are reporting powerful increases in employee
engagement, communication, positive interactions, and collaboration between individuals, within teams, and across business units. The results are both local and systemwide.

On quantitative measures, teams, business units, and companies are scoring significantly higher on multiple measures on company surveys, including customer satisfaction.

On financial measures, business units are showing gains in financial results; sales are rising by double digits; companies are retaining key leaders; and in one company, "increased trust and communication saved a $1m. error."

On the professional level, leaders are scoring higher on 360^0 surveys, and there are multiple instances where leaders using the Enneagram for their development have been promoted 2-3 levels higher within very short time periods.

Surprise 2 | MAGNIFIER EFFECT

Many interviewees described how the Enneagram spreads within a company, and one leader specifically used the term *Magnifier Effect*: "The positive impact and spread of the Enneagram gets magnified; the Enneagram's applications are limitless in what they can do for organizations."

Surprise 3 | HIGH ENTHUSIASM

Interviewees report that once employees learn the Enneagram, they want more and more. They share it with friends, take it with them to new companies, and bring it home: "At company events, spouses talk about how it has helped their family. No one ever says that about a finance class."

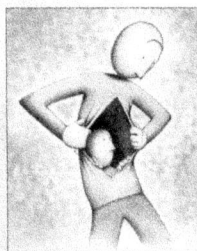

RESULTS: *"Tangible results occur within 6 months, but sustainable results take a year or longer. It's like going to the gym. At first, you feel tired but better. After a while, you feel much better, then think you don't need to go anymore. However, you have to use it regularly to experience its full contribution. The longer you use the Enneagram, the more benefits; it becomes 2nd nature to you and the organization."*

TRENDS
what to expect in the future

Introduction

Based on the data collected, these are the trends we expect to see in the future.

Trend 1 | Stage of Innovation

Our research shows that the Enneagram's use in organizations is in the *early adopter* stage of innovation (see shaded area on graph), but the companies currently using the Enneagram vary overall from *innovators* to *laggards*. The clear message: even if your company is not an innovator, you can be! How? In all 72 companies studied, the Enneagram has been introduced and championed by a person of credibility and respect – a leader, HR professional, coach, or consultant – who "sees the big picture and understands how the Enneagram complements and supports the outcomes critical to the organization's success."

Innovation

Innovators (2.5%)

Early Adopters (13.5%)

Early Majority (34%)

Late Majority (34%)

Laggards (16%)

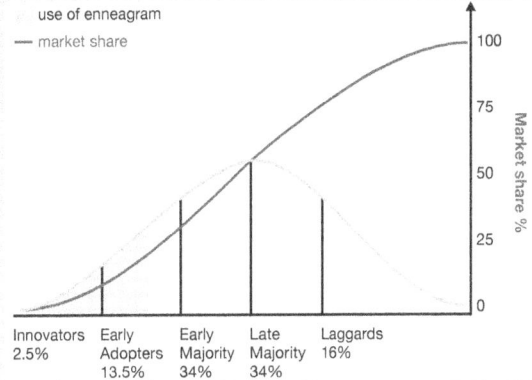

Innovators are organizations that are forward-looking, risk-takers who employ innovative approaches without needing the reassurance of others: *early adopters* ask who else is doing this and take the risk once companies they admire have done it first; *early majority* includes organizations that don't want to be left behind; *late majority* organizations do something only after it has been tried and proven; and *laggards* are organizations that may never come onboard.

To utilize innovation to increase market share, organizations need to be among the first 50% of adopters (by *early majority*). This model, *Diffusion of Innovations*, was developed in 1962 by Everett M. Rogers.

Trend 2 | Length of Time for Results

The answer to this question was both clear and ambiguous: *it depends*. The more these variables are present, the faster the results: resource commitment (time, financial, leadership sponsorship); consultant expertise; relevancy of the work to important business needs; cultural fit (development orientation); breadth and depth of applications; follow-up and reinforcement. Business challenges that are large in size and scope require more time, whereas work with teams and individuals requires less.

Trend 3 | The Enneagram's Next Wave

An increasing number of companies will be using the Enneagram, as it spreads laterally within organizations and also moves globally from its current *early adopter* to *early majority* users. Expect an increase in the Enneagram's credibility, legitimacy, and visibility via research, evidence-based success stories, case studies, and use in academic institutions, including business schools.

Post-Changing Checklist

It is so important to do a post-consulting phase review to make sure that everything that needed doing was accomplished well and/or to identify areas that still need attention before moving forward in the consultation.

For each changing topic below, rate yourself (3) well done; (2) needs more work; or (1) didn't do much and needs lots of attention. For items given a 1 or 2 rating, write down what you need to do prior to or during the next client meeting.

CHANGING TOPIC	RATING	NEED TO DO
Change areas identified and prioritized		
Client takes clear ownership for the change and is committed to take action		
Viable action plan created		
Design for the change activities carefully done and materials needed professionally delivered		
Client used consultant(s) effectively without being overly-dependent on them		
Chosen intervention(s) to address the change areas implemented successfully		
Tangible and intangible positive results have occurred as a result of the change effort		
Change activities (from action plan) were implemented flexibly so that adjustments were made to original plan (if needed)		
Client is satisfied with the results		
Consultant(s) learned something new		
If a consulting team, the team worked well together on behalf of the client		

CHAPTER 8
CLOSING | CONSULTING with THE ENNEAGRAM

If you want a happy ending, that depends, of course, on where you stop your story.
Orson Wells

Closing conversations are often avoided, but so important. Closing requires a discussion about being finished with the consulting project and the client-consultant relationship or having to deal with unfinished work or interpersonal issues. Closing involves separation, and it requires attention and honesty. Even if there is a strong probability of continued work together, it is still the end of one phase and onto a new one. The following materials can guide you through the Closing Stage.

Closing and the Enneagram

Balanced scorecard

Post-closing checklist

Closing and the Enneagram

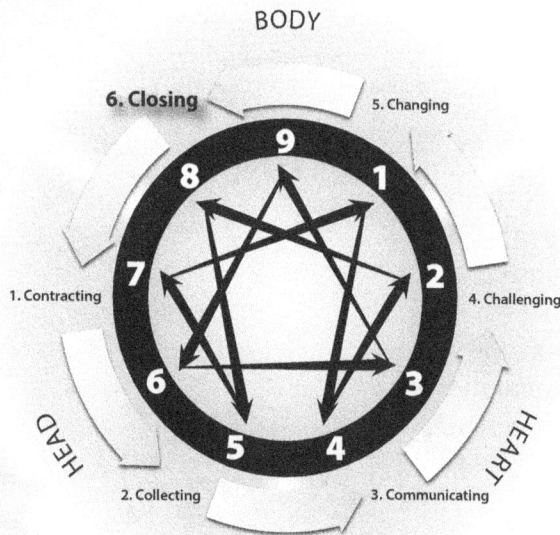

BODY

6. Closing

5. Changing

8   9   1

7   2

1. Contracting   4. Challenging

HEAD   6   3   HEART

5   4

2. Collecting   3. Communicating

What is the best way to assess what results were achieved, including the client's intended goals, but also any unanticipated outcomes?

To what extent do the client and the consultant both feel satisfied with the consultation?

What can be learned from this work?

Is there more left to do, and if so, who does it; if not, how do we say "good-bye?"

Is the client (and organization) fully equipped to follow-on with the results of the consultation so that the results are anchored and, therefore, sustainable?

Is there a need to re-contract, and if so, what is the nature of the engagement?

Were we able to bring psychological as well as task-related closure to the consulting engagement?

During the *Closing* Stage of the consultation, there are both task-related challenges and relationship-based ones. The tasks are relatively straightforward. Were the intended outcomes accomplished and to what degree? How was or will the results be measured to know for certain? Are client and consultant both satisfied with what was done? Is there more to do to ensure the change effort's longevity and sustainability? What important lessons were learned and can be carried into the future for both the client and consultant? And while the contract may be over, is there more consulting needed, and if so, what? Finally, what more does the client need in order to go forward with the change, whether or not the consultant maintains some sort of involvement?

The relationship issues are also straightforward, but because they involve feelings, ending a consulting engagement can be an emotional challenge for both the client and consultant. If the consultation was successful, it is likely that most clients and consultants will be experiencing both joy/satisfaction and relief. The joy and satisfaction come from having accomplished something important. This deserves expression and even celebration, and the consultant can encourage rituals of celebration with either the client or those in the client system most closely impacted. Relief is almost always present to some degree. Change efforts take time, focus, and energy, and it can be a relief to have the change initiative over so the energy can be directed elsewhere. At the end of successful consultations, there is also usually both sadness and appreciation related to closing the relationship between the client and consultant, especially if there is no specific follow-on work that involves the consultant. It is a separation that needs acknowledgment. Will the client bring this up? Not normally, so it is important that the consultant has the emotional sensitivity to know that this is important to discuss and is willing to bring up the subject at the right time and place.

If the consultation has been more difficult, an in-depth closing conversation is essential. Here are some examples: the consultation didn't produce the expected results; the client and consultant never really worked well together; the client or the consultant harbors some negative feelings toward the other, but these never got sufficiently expressed and resolved; both the client and consultant gave the work their best, but something beyond their control went wrong – for example, organizational resources for the project were no longer available due to budgetary constraints or decisions made at higher levels in the organization; and the list could go on. Discussing these difficult issues needs to be done carefully and only to the extent that there is sufficient closure. The idea is to bring enough understanding and acceptance to what was or might have been, and to do so without recrimination (either of self or other). If this difficult conversation is avoided, the issues and unanswered questions will continue in the minds and hearts of both the client and consultant in ways that serve neither well.

Enneagram Insights

Separations, endings, and new beginnings are often a challenge for many people, no matter what their Enneagram style. Dealing effectively with both the tasks and relationship aspects of the *Closing* Stage adds even more complexity to the situation, and this is true for both the client and the consultant. The following Enneagram insights refer to both the client and the consultant in this final stage of the consultation.

Ones

Ones tend to be more comfortable with tasks than the nuances of relationships and feelings, but many Ones are quite sentimental and can become emotional in surprising ways. Ending a supportive and fulfilling relationship can elicit strong affectionate emotions that even surprise them. It is so important to allow the time and space for this. If the consultation has had problems, however, discussing them at this stage may feel like a fruitless endeavor because nothing can be done at this point to improve anything, and Ones are all about making improvement. "It can always be better" doesn't seem to apply at the end, and yet it does. Better to discuss difficult issues in a respectful and honest way than to have them linger afterward as regrets or resentments.

Twos

Twos may have a desire and a tendency to discuss the relationship issues at the *Closing* Stage more than they want or need to discuss the task-related issues such as deliverables and specific results, but it is so important to bring closure to both task and relationship issues. It can help Twos if there is a specific agenda of topics to discuss so that both the task and the relationship issues at the *Closing* Stage get equal attention.

Threes

Whether the consultant or the client, Threes often end up feeling very close to the other person when a consultation has been challenging and successful. In a sense, a bond of intimacy develops that many Threes find heart opening in a way they may not experience very often in their own personal and professional lives. What better way to develop closeness than working together on a shared project in an honest and open relationship? For this reason, however, the separation involved in ending a consultation may be painful to some Threes. They may avoid any discussion of it, go headlong into activity to avoid feeling sad, or they may joke about it as a way to discharge their feelings. They may even try to prolong the work as a way of maintaining the connection. It is far better is to discuss the separation issues directly. Then, it is very clear that any follow-on work or re-contracting is absolutely needed rather than being used as a way to not end the consulting relationship.

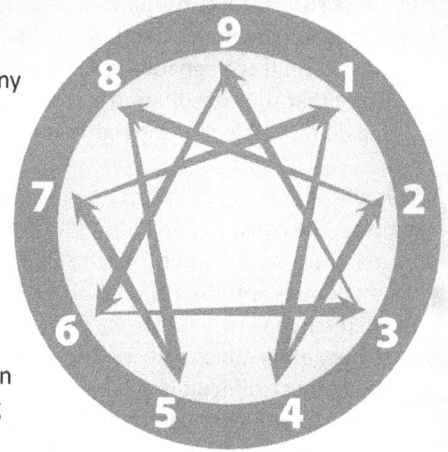

Fours

Fours almost always find endings and separations emotionally difficult since separation after closeness can feel like abandonment and trigger deeply sad feelings in them. At the same time, most Fours are aware of this and feel a need to discuss these feelings and related issues so they don't keep replaying them in their hearts. In fact, they may want to discuss the issues longer and deeper than non-Fours, so here is where a balance must be found between emotional expression and moving on.

Fives

Fives don't like to appear soft or sentimental, but when closeness develops in a consulting relationship, Fives can feel as attached to the human connection and as reluctant to separate as individuals of any Enneagram style. On the other hand, once the feelings are expressed in a true way, most Fives are ready for a change of topic and to move onto a less soft subject. A Five who has done a great deal of self-development work may bring up the subject without hesitation; a Five with less self-development may not initiate a conversation about separation, but he or she will likely engage in the dialogue.

Sixes

Most Sixes are extremely sentimental (think of it as emotional loyalty) and when they trust the other person in a consulting relationship, there will be anxiety about separation and "letting go." As a result, this anxiety, as well as affection, needs to be discussed in the *Closing* Stage of the consultation. Otherwise, Sixes will play and replay their feelings and reactions for a very long time, thus needlessly tying up their energy. In addition, there may be either some fear or fearlessness related to the tasks still unfinished, if there are any. These also need to be discussed so that the Six neither avoids what must be done nor rushes rashly into action.

Sevens

Because Sevens avoid sadness and prefer to stay away from fear, the *Closing* Stage may predictably be something from which Sevens run away. Here are some of the ways of avoidance: not showing up for the meeting or showing up, but exhibiting behaviors that distract from the discussion – for example, changing the subject, telling jokes, sharing prolonged stories, or presenting a new issue of interest as a substitute for the ending and separation discussion. It is so important to bring closure in the consulting relationship, to deal with sadness caused by separation so they don't linger subliminally, and to examine real and not-so-real fears in order to address them and move forward.

Eights

Eights can really be teddy bears when it comes to separation and relationships. Tender and tough, they will have an open and honest discussion about this, even though they may feel vulnerable in doing so. This can be quite healing, so make sure to allow the time and space for it. However, if the Eight was dissatisfied with the consultation, they will need to be able to express their displeasure as well. Behind the dissatisfaction may lay some feelings of appreciation.

Nines

Nines may or may not be aware that they are having feelings related to separation. The reason for this is that Nines tend to merge with others (as well as things and processes), so separation in the consulting relationship may tear at their sense of connectivity and well being. The intensity of this reaction to separation may not be in their own conscious awareness, the result of a coping strategy. The best way through this is to discuss the issues and feelings in a clear, respectful and practical way, which includes specifics of what further contact between you two might entail, even if it's an occasional email or phone call.

The End

Balanced Scorecard

The Balanced Scorecard as a method of measuring results arose from the work of Kaplan and Norton (The Balanced Scorecard, Harvard Business Review Press, 1996). Rather than assessing results based on short or medium financial performance – or any other single performance factor – the Balanced Scorecard suggests the four factors (goals and outcomes) depicted in the model.

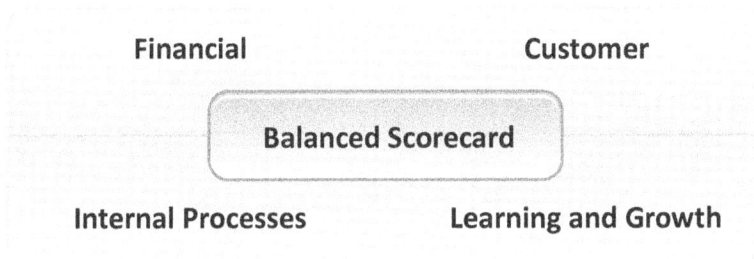

Financial   **Customer**

> **Balanced Scorecard**

Internal Processes   **Learning and Growth**

In the original model, all four performance factors are given equal weight, but rearranging these same four factors suggests more of a hierarchy of importance.

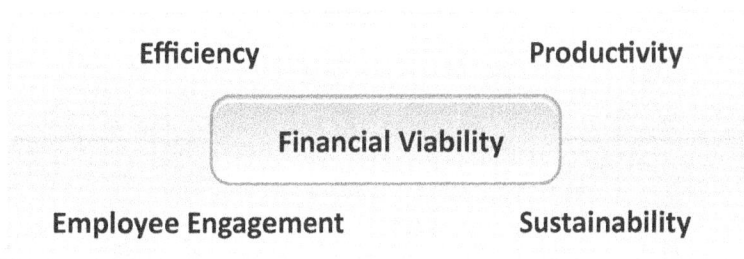

Financial

Customer

Internal Processes

Learning and Growth

Efficiency   **Productivity**

> **Financial Viability**

Employee Engagement   **Sustainability**

In addition to changing the hierarchical value of the factors, you can also change the number of factors as well as the factors themselves.

The challenge or question, after the factors have been determined, is how to measure them.

Post-Closing Checklist

It is so important to do a post-consulting phase review to make sure that everything that needed doing was accomplished well and/or to identify areas that still need attention even though the consultation is officially finished.

For each closing topic below, rate yourself (3) well done; (2) needs more work; or (1) didn't do much and needs lots of attention. For items given a 1 or 2 rating, write down what you need to do to bring complete closure to the consultation.

CLOSING TOPIC	RATING	NEED TO DO
Goals (outcomes) and deliverables accomplished		
Results assessment agreed upon		
Sustainability of change effectively discussed and planned		
New issues discussed and resolved		
Client equipped to go forward without the consultant(s)		
Discussion of lessons learned		
Closure brought to project mentally and emotionally		
Closing ritual included		
Re-contracting needed and agreed to		

CHAPTER 9
CONSULTANT DEVELOPMENT | CONSULTING with
THE ENNEAGRAM

We are looking for the key to our ultimate fulfillment in the wrong place.
Claudio Naranjo

Consultants, hopefully, recognize that their own personal
and professional development contribute to the success of
their consultation projects. They become less reactive, more
responsive, less assumptive, more objective, less constrained,
and more real. The following items support the growth and
development of consultants:

Strengths and development areas

How to use consulting for
your own development

Consultants | Consulting Strengths and Development Areas

HEAD CENTER STYLES	STRENGTHS	DEVELOPMENT AREAS
5	Conceptual abilities and model-building; remains steady in chaotic circumstances; grasps multiple dimensions of reality; broad view of what is occurring; patient; roots for others' success; objective; excellent content knowledge (even about process); excellent at planning and well thought-out action	Marketing (has trouble putting self "out there"); following up in ambiguous situations; leads with mind and may have difficulty with the affective in the here and now; may be perceived as cool, distant, and detached; tends to overdo complexity and conceptual models; may not be a team player
6	Grounded; pragmatic; thinks quickly on feet; plans for multiple contingencies; loyal; experience-based and able to relate experience to client's experience; intuitive; honest; high degree of integrity; sustains relationships; sharp focus; not easily deceived	May tend to see primarily the worst case scenario; often has high anxiety or is overly concerned about outcomes (before or after the fact); hard work and focus often occur under pressure; may project concerns, feelings, and anxieties onto client; low tolerance for ambiguity; may overuse the "tried and true"
7	Quick; intuitive; bonds quickly; spontaneous; creative with new ideas and new ways of doing things; connects unlike ideas; creates sense of optimism and enjoyment in the client system; good initiator; energetic	Impatient; tends to have short term client relationships (goes in and out of client systems readily); stronger in conception than implementation; tends to shy away from systematic structure; rationalizes criticism; may collude in avoiding organizational pain; may implement change for the sake of change

Consultants | Consulting Strengths and Development Areas

HEART CENTER STYLES	STRENGTHS	DEVELOPMENT AREAS
2	Relates well to all types of people in client system; affectively sensitive; excellent interpersonal skills (in 1-on-1s and group settings); highly likable; generous with time and energy; elicits in-depth information from client about client system; helpful; works well in consulting teams; compassionate and non-judgmental	Saying "no" to client (regarding time, decisions, etc.); anxiety in terms of how they "come across" and if people like them; may have trouble in groups about how to act (because they may act differently with different individuals); may not step up to the task of providing leadership (assertion); may have trouble in a non-supportive environment; may increase client dependence
3	Able to be "on" in small and large group interactions even when they feel "off"; generates confidence; excellent at accomplishing tasks; strong in project management; hardworking and high-achieving; pragmatic; results oriented; good leader (client and consulting team); adapts well; efficient; energetic	May feel continuously depleted from work after having performed well; anxiety after each performance and success; impatient with process and "feeling" issues; over-identified with work (not enough separation); may take a real consulting failure as a deep level of self failure; may compete with client; may come across as insincere
4	Honest; forthright; empathic; strives for excellent work; develops close and trusting relationships with clients quickly and easily; good at highly challenging projects; creative; intuitive; helps clients get to core issues; strong in conflict resolution; good critical thinkers; idealistic; works well in arena of meaning	May take events or criticism (particularly if negative) too personally; may get too emotionally concerned about the client; stands up directly for what is right when a less direct approach may be more effective; not a good team player when conflict areas are left unresolved; personal responses may color objectivity; may get bored when not highly emotionally engaged

Consultants | Consulting Strengths and Development Areas

BODY CENTER STYLES	STRENGTHS	DEVELOPMENT AREAS
8	Generates confidence from the client system; energetic; outgoing; assertive (willing to state directly concerns and objections); committed; excellent at project management; honest; minimizes ambiguity for client; willing to deal with conflict; hard working; sees big picture; charismatic; can take action when action is needed	May be too direct with client; may not see multiple sides of an issue (particularly when emotions or values are involved); may be perceived as inappropriately controlling; may not control anger with a client; may overextend; critical of weakness (in client system, consulting team members)
9	Mediation; building relationships with all types of people; good interpersonal skills; calming demeanor; can understand/value/consolidate multiple points of view; orderly; makes people feel comfortable; steady; inclusive; fair-minded	May avoid or have aversion to conflict; may have difficulty helping clients sort priorities and delegate; difficulty disagreeing or taking a strong position with a client; may not see outside conventional patterns of behavior
1	Exacting; ability to manage the nuts and bolts of a project from beginning to end; demand the highest quality in all aspects of consulting; eye for detail; inner aesthetic sense of when a consultation goes perfectly; ability to grasp fundamental core client issues; ability to keep a team "on task"; tenacity	Judgmental toward client or co-consultant when he or she makes mistakes; heavily self-critical when project doesn't go just right; tendency toward flares of anger toward client (particularly when value system gets violated); controlling; focus on "trees" rather than "forest"; difficulty taking feedback; may be inflexible

Consultants | How to Use Consulting for Your Own Development

There are also ways in which consultants can use the client-consultant interactions for their own development. This is not intended to suggest that the consultant put these items on the consulting agenda as doing so would create some role confusion – the client might end up consulting the consultant. Consequently, consultants should work on their own issues by themselves, although they should feel free to ask clients for periodic feedback about either the consulting in general or any of the following items below.

HEAD CENTER STYLES

5
The objectivity that most Five consultants bring to consulting is a great asset, since clients – including Five clients – are rarely able to look at themselves and their situations objectively by themselves. Five consultants do, however, need to pay close attention to their own display of warmth so that they do not appear overly cerebral or analytic to their clients. Consulting is a human interaction, and Five consultants need to be able to elicit and pursue the emotional reactions of their clients.

Paying attention to the feeling side of organizations is also important when Five consultants listen to or give advice to clients regarding interactions with others or work-related planning. Fives might err, for example, in emphasizing project planning but minimizing the importance of getting buy-in from those directly affected by the project. Fives should also remember to leverage their strengths, such as understanding cause and effect, seeing how the different parts of issues fit together, and remaining calm in times of duress.

6
Sixes bring great strengths as consultants, and they are often quite humble about these assets – for example, consulting leverages the Six's skills in developing relationships, understanding how organizations work, planning, and raising important issues.

On the other hand, Six consultants need to pay attention to three areas in particular: (1) their worry or anxiety about something may spill over into their work with a client; (2) they may influence the client to plan excessively; and (3) they may convey a can't-do attitude to their clients when, in reality, a can-do orientation would be far more helpful. Clients are usually anxious enough themselves when they pursue consulting, and they want their consultants to be self-assured. Also, clients may tend to overplan when they feel anxious, and they often need to have the consultant guide them toward self-reflection before developing action plans. Consulting thus provides Six consultants with an excellent opportunity to use their strengths and work on their own growth.

7
While Seven clients may avoid or delay their consulting meetings, this is not usually the case for Seven consultants. Sevens often enjoy consulting, both because it provides variety in their work lives and because they often find their clients to be quite interesting. In return, clients may appreciate Seven consultants for their ideas and optimism.

A caution, however, for Sevens is to make certain that the focus of the consulting is on the client's needs and development. Seven consultants, for example, may tell stories from their own experience as a way of demonstrating empathy or suggesting a course of action, but they may talk longer than needed, thus deflecting attention away from the client. Or, Seven consultants may make many exciting suggestions to the client, when instead they should ask clients for their own ideas first. Seven consultants are at their best when they use their strengths and also stay focused on the client and on the consulting goals.

Consultant Development | 137

HEART CENTER STYLES

2 Because Two consultants usually enjoy consulting – it offers them a chance to help others – they often become quite involved with their clients, showing great concern during the consulting meeting and keeping in contact with clients between meetings. A caution for Two consultants, however, is to keep in mind that the ultimate goal of consulting is to help the client to become independent of the consultant. The close relationship that Two consultants often develop with their clients can actually create an unproductive degree of dependency in the client.

In addition, Two consultants need to pay attention to their reactions to their clients. When working with clients they like, Two consultants may give the clients too much benefit of the doubt rather than confronting them when needed. On the other hand, when Two consultants don't like clients or feel frustrated by them, they may become insistent and harsh when giving negative feedback, or they may even "fire" the client.

Two consultants often become role models for clients and can leverage their strengths toward this end – for example, their strengths in developing relationships, demonstrating warmth and understanding, and being empathic.

3 While Three consultants are usually adept at consulting for results – the ultimate objective of the consulting process – they need to pay equal attention to the process by which these results are achieved. Paying attention to process means helping clients to deal with their feelings and examine multiple options for achieving their desired results – Threes may have a bias to achieving results in the most expedient way – and allowing time during the consulting to discuss the relationship between the consultant and the client. Three consultants may also want to take on the additional challenge of consulting some clients who do not fit their idea of a confident, successful person. Doing so challenges Three consultants to look at themselves and their own responses, and it pushes them to deal with their own issues of competence and image.

4 Four consultants often work with clients at deep levels of understanding, leveraging their ability to make connection with others as a basis for moving the consulting process forward. While this can be invaluable to many clients, there will be other clients who do not want to talk about deeper feelings, personal values, and issues of life's purpose. They may simply want someone whom they can talk to and who will help them develop practical ideas for action.

A second caution for Four consultants is to stay focused on the client's consulting goals. Four consultants can become so enamored of their discussions with clients about feelings and the consulting relationship that they may lessen the movement toward results. Fours can also make good use of their ability to bring out the best in others and their willingness to explore at difficult issues.

BODY CENTER STYLES

8   Eight consultants are usually helpful role models for clients, particularly in the areas of personal strength and power. Their sensitivity to organizational politics and their ability to assert themselves are traits that many consulting clients want to emulate. On the other hand, because Eights often mask their own vulnerabilities and have an aversion to people they perceive as weaklings, they may shy away from clients who appear anxious or uncertain. Even confident people feel anxious and uncertain at times, and consulting clients are often dealing with issues that cause them to feel fearful or to appear unsure of themselves. Thus, being a consultant can be a challenge for some Eights.

In addition, Eights tend to be decisive, whereas a client may feel hesitant or tentative about a decision that he or she needs to make. Eights need to restrain themselves from telling clients what to do, instead eliciting possible options and consequences from the client.

9   Clients usually enjoy their consulting sessions with the Nine consultant because most Nines are easy to relate to and are, at least externally, nonjudgmental. The challenge for Nine consultants, however, is to keep the pace of the consulting session moving in a way that propels the client toward action. While the Nine's tendency to understand a situation from alternative points of view can be enormously useful to clients, who often see things only from their own perspective, the Nine consultant must also help the client to determine which point or points of view are the most valid and useful.

At certain times, clients will also want to know where the consultant stands and what he or she thinks. Because this may require the consultant to confront the client, Nine consultants will be personally challenged in such situations.

Nines need to remember three things: (1) the client values both them and their opinions; (2) their practical, concrete suggestions can be extremely helpful; and (3) take the risk to be assertive because it will benefit both you and the client.

1   Consulting provides the opportunity for One consultants to work on their tendencies to be critical of the client's behavior; to become impatient with the client's progress, trying to move the consulting conversations quickly; and to focus on the task so intently that their warmth does not come across to the client. These growth opportunities are likely to arise for One consultants during every consulting meeting. One consultants should try to remind themselves of their strengths, such as their skills in analysis and discernment as well as their action orientation. After a consulting meeting, as the consultant reflects on the interaction and progress, it can be very helpful to think about all of the things that went well, rather than focusing primarily on all the things that could have gone better.

CHAPTER 10
CASE STUDIES | CONSULTING with THE ENNEAGRAM

Experience without theory is blind, but theory without experience is mere intellectual play.
Immanuel Kant

The three case studies in this section illuminate the 6-C consulting process in action. Sometimes simple and sometimes complex, they represent three different examples of how following a systematic consulting process offers the best client results, often beyond what the client and consultant initially planned. The consulting process is linear yet iterative, uses a structure while learning as you go, and involves reflecting on this experience to increase the capabilities of both the client and the consultant for future work.

Case Study 1 | Transforming Leadership Culture
by Ginger Lapid-Bogda PhD

Case Study 2 | The Multi-faceted Consultation
by Matt Ahrens MBA

Case Study 3 | Social Intelligence Hiring
by Ginger Lapid-Bogda PhD

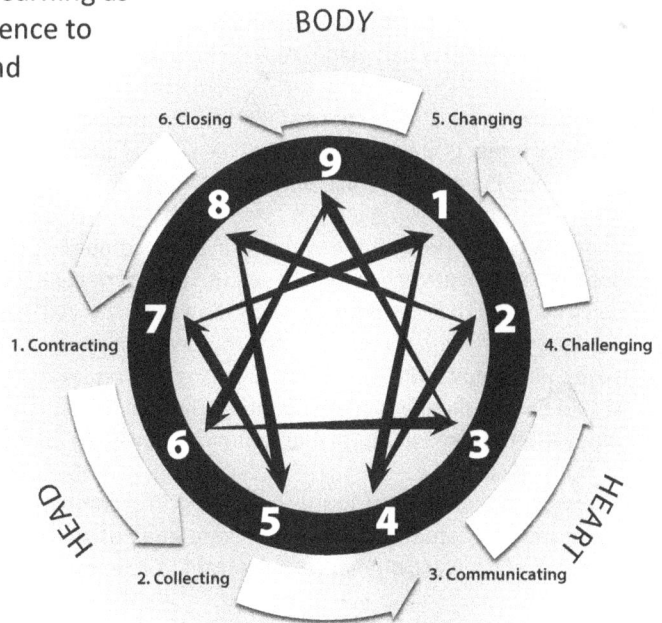

Case Studies | Transforming Leadership Culture
by Ginger Lapid-Bogda PhD

Context

Life-Saving, Inc. (a pseudonym) is known for its firm commitment to producing life-enhancing drugs, often drugs that no other pharmaceutical company is willing to create. Life-Saving, and its IT (Information Technology) function in particular, has had a deep commitment to the development of all its employees, often winning prestigious awards as the most desirable place to work. With an eye on the strategic and long-term importance of leadership development, the head of IT (Terry, an Enneagram 7 and an advocate of the developmental aspects of the Enneagram) decided to launch an Enneagram-leadership initiative based on linking the Enneagram to specific leadership competencies.

Contracting

Terry's initial request to Ginger, the consultant and an Enneagram 2, was clear and simple: develop a competency-based leadership development program using the Enneagram that would transform the 135 managers in IT over a year's period of time into top quality leaders who achieved results and were also visionary, strategic, strong operationally, committed to their own development, and excellent people developers. As an Enneagram 7, Terry had many ideas on how to do this, and he wanted a lot done in a short time.

Having worked with him successfully on prior projects, his consultant was used to helping Terry sort through complex projects with a multitude of ideas, plus adding others of her own. As an Enneagram 2, listening to his needs, helping discern which ones might work, and developing an implementation strategy came easily.

There were two problems, however. First, the company's corporate training group, not known for being either speedy or innovative, had been given the task of developing a system-wide leadership development program. Terry guessed that, based on past performance, it would take corporate training two to three years to develop a program, and it was not likely that this creation would be innovative. As an Enneagram 7 – for example, liking speed and innovation – Terry was unwilling to wait, even knowing that the politics of moving ahead on his own would be a challenge. And he doubted whether the end product would be innovative, saying this: "How much innovation can you get from a program developed by committee?"

The second problem was more challenging. The company was currently using five different leadership frameworks created by different vendors, some of which used similar but not identical competency areas and some of which were dramatically different in orientation. Which would he choose?

As a result, the contracting became very specific and highly strategic. The deliverable would be monthly leadership development "Learning Communities" of leaders from intact management teams, with a different leadership competency integrated with the Enneagram each month. The exact structure of these "Learning

Communities" as well as the leadership competencies themselves and how they would be integrated with the Enneagram would be determined after the data collection and data feedback were complete.

The data collection process was agreed upon as follows: Terry would get the consultant every leadership framework being used in any way and any information on the progress (or lack of it) from corporate training. From this information, the consultant would do an analysis of overlaps and discrepancies between and among the different frameworks to share and discuss with Terry. Information on the progress of corporate training would be information only at this point to be used later in developing an effective strategy.

Collecting

Collecting data from the five assorted leadership development competency frameworks involved using the organization's documents as well as going to the various vendors' websites for more detail. The result was confusing and complicated. Nine of the frameworks had the same leadership competencies listed; in fact only three competencies emerged among all five frameworks – for example, drive for results, leading teams, and communication – but the different frameworks didn't define these three competencies the same way. In addition, some of the competencies from one framework were sub-sets or sub-descriptions under another competency. Even more, there were some obvious competency areas missing – for example, developing self-mastery, thinking and leading strategically, and decision making.

The documents related to the corporate training group's work on leadership development was unremarkable. Although they'd been meeting for over a year, they had only clarified the parameters of their charter and the logistics of their meetings.

From Ginger's perspective as a consultant, the data was clearly confusing with no obvious action that could be taken from the data as it was. As an Enneagram 2, she was concerned about how she could add value, how she could best serve her client and the larger client system – specifically, the organization's leaders – and how she could keep her client and herself out of trouble with the organization given that the corporate training function was known to be territorial.

Communicating | data feedback

The diagnostic summary of the five different frameworks appeared crucial. The problem was that there was so much confusing data since these frameworks work both dissimilar and overlapping. To solve this issue, Ginger created a multipage document with a grid showing each framework, its strengths and weaknesses, the overlaps between and among the five frameworks, which competencies appeared in subsections of another framework, and what competency areas were available that were not included at all. All of this was color-coded so Terry could see it all at a glance. Sevens like to skim to get the gist of a situation rather going into elaborate detail. Ginger prepared the data so it told the story within a five-minute review.

The conversation regarding the frameworks with Terry went better than Ginger expected, partly due to the data presentation but also a result of the fact that the data told him what he already sensed. Although the data showed Terry and Ginger had much more work to do than anticipated, the tasks ahead became clear.

The conversation regarding the corporate training group was difficult because it was actually worse than Terry anticipated. They showed a great deal of activity and emails of activity but no action whatsoever.

While these challenges might be daunting to some, they were not for Terry and Ginger. Terry had been convinced that the key to changing the culture of IT was changing the way leaders led. He wanted them to step up into and stay in leadership.

Challenging

The challenge for Terry and Ginger was simply this: to make a thoughtful "go" or "no go" decision on this project. There were two major issues involved. The first issue was how important this effort was to Terry as a leader of leaders. How central was developing leadership in his IT function? Whether the project used the Enneagram or not, there would be a lot of work involved and a great deal of attention would need to be paid to how to work the interface or relationship with corporate training group, particularly because they could feel extremely threatened by the work and undercut Terry's efforts.

The second issue related to a calculation regarding the chances for success or failure (the risk/reward ratio) and how much effort and how many resources – time, money, information – would be required to optimize the chances for success. Were the required resources available?

While the two issues above may have seemed daunting in terms of risk and effort, Terry and Ginger believed it was both a challenge worth facing and an exciting prospect. First, Terry decided he was 100% committed to leadership development as central to his organizational change strategy moving from disengagement and silos to full engagement and collaboration. As an Enneagram 7 and rebellious by nature, he didn't believe in the words "No" or "You can't." In fact, a "NO" often fueled him forward. As an Enneagram 2, Ginger was oriented both to helping Terry achieve success and to the nearly 150 leaders who would benefit from the project. They decided they would rise or fall together on this project.

Changing | action planning and implementation

Once the decision to move forward with the project was made, the action plans actually came easily. There were two major prongs to the plan, each which intersected with the other.

Leadership development with the Enneagram

Terry, with Ginger's consultation, selected seven leadership competencies he thought most crucial, electing among them the three that appear on all given prior leadership frameworks. The reasoning was simple; these were three competencies that the training group would likely select as their competencies and, as a result, selecting these three competency areas – drive for results, communication and teams – would align us with the future work of the training group. And because the training group had done no work on these yet, Terry and Ginger reasoned that they could develop these three areas themselves.

For the remaining four competency areas, Terry decided that he could pick what he wanted, then convince corporate training later on that these were good ideas. He selected, based on thought and conversation, these: strategy, decision-making, change, and self-mastery. What, he reasoned, could be wrong with these.

Ginger then designed the leadership development program in terms of "learning communities of leaders," where each intact management team spent four hours each month meeting to (a) learn the competency; (b) discuss their Enneagram-based strengths and development areas in relation to the competency; (c) engage in an exciting competency-based skill-building activity; and (d) discuss how to support one another's growth. Ginger facilitated each "learning community" in collaboration with the team's manager for a year. Word spread quickly how exciting and relaxing these sessions were, and the growth of almost every leader involved was obvious to themselves and others.

Aligning with corporate training

Aligning with corporate training was, surprisingly, the easiest part of the project. Because they were so far behind yet had concrete deliverables looming, they actually appreciated that a high level leader was so interested. Terry shared the first three competencies, but gave the exact names suggested by corporate training. This made them think the competencies were theirs, not Terry's, plus they could take credit for the success of the work he did. Even more, Terry fed them the competency information for the remaining four areas as they were created. Less work for corporate training, and a big win for them!

Why did not getting the credit for all this work bother neither Terry nor Ginger? The Enneagram provides insight here. Both Terry and Ginger are social subtypes. As a social subtype 7 (called "sacrifice"), Terry's focus was on getting something significant to happen based on innovative ideas and he was not motivated by getting credit for what he had done, sacrificing his own need for recognition on behalf of the initiative. As a social subtype 2 (called "ambition"), Ginger's motivation was to make something big and important happen for which she would derive a sense of her own contribution without having to take direct credit for it.

Closing | Assessment, institutionalization of the change, and separation

The project was successful beyond expectation. At the individual level, leaders who participated in it made large developmental changes within the first four months of the program. They became more aware and self-accepting, but also made developmental leaps based on their Enneagram types. For example, the Nine leaders became more assertive, Eight leaders became more vulnerable and receptive, Five leaders became more emotional and integrated, and so on. At the team level, the management teams became more cohesive, more supportive of one another, increasingly honest in their interactions, and far more trusting. At the cultural level, the shift was even more dramatic. The entire management culture shifted to one in which leaders took responsibility for their work performance as well as their personal and professional development. The Enneagram made it easy for them to do so because the developmental activities are customized by type to specific developmental areas. Even more important, the leadership culture changed form one of self-protection and competition to openness and support and the organizational culture shifted to one in which all points of view and work styles are valued.

To sustain this leadership development initiative, other programs and approaches were selectively added. All employees were offered attendance – completely voluntary – at a one-day Enneagram program; participation was close to 95% of the 500 employees. Thus, leaders were able to use the Enneagram to develop the individuals and teams for which they were responsible. A robust Enneagram website was created that hosted multiple Enneagram items designed for deeper learning – for example, 45-minute Enneagram type panels with 5 people of each type being interviewed as a panel; an interaction matrix where leaders and individual employees could click on any two Enneagram type numbers and learn how they interacted with peers, when in a boss-employee relationship, and during a performance review, as well as development ideas to make each of these interactions more effective.

As an Enneagram 7, Terry was thrilled with the result. From his idea, an entire transformation occurred. And, as a 7, he was happy being "hands-off" when it came to producing the deliverable implementation. As an Enneagram 2, this appealed to Ginger who could become creative and expansive in this high-impact project.

Conclusion

This project's impact has continued, years after its inception. The Enneagram's use spread throughput the organization, far beyond the IT function. The robust website was available to everyone in the organization. With the Enneagram, almost anything is possible, but it is new territory, giving those who pursue it the opportunity to create and construct. It does take resources more than time, as positive results are often seen within months, but providing the peripherals to support the work, plus visible support from leadership, are essential ingredients.

Case Studies | The Multi-faceted Consultation
by Matt Ahrens MBA

Context

Silicon Valley Tech ("SVT," a pseudonym) is a fast growing, 10-year-old company specializing in a specialty technology. SVT recently hired Roger Jones, an Enneagram 8, as its first Chief Information Officer (CIO) to run the Information Technology (IT) department. Roger inherited Chris Smith, an Enneagram 1, who prior to Roger's hire managed IT from a Senior Director level position. Reporting to Chris was a high potential Director, Neil Clark, an Enneagram 6, who also had a dotted line reporting relationship to Roger – the first such reporting relationship in the company. Roger believed that Neil would benefit from some coaching in order to continue advancing in his career and was referred to Matt, an Enneagram 9.

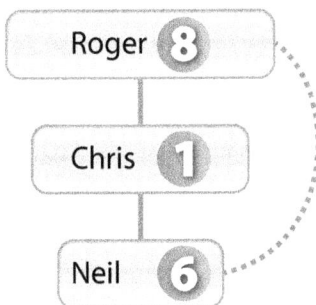

Contracting

The introduction was made between Roger and Matt via email. Roger replied, saying he wanted the coaching to begin as soon as possible and that he could speak with Matt when he returned from a business trip in a week. He then brokered an email introduction between Neil and Matt. Neil, in turn, brokered an email introduction to Chris, informing Matt that Chris would be getting coaching too. Matt had initial meetings with both Neil and Chris individually prior to speaking directly to Roger. They each wanted to receive a 360-feedback review and told Matt that Roger said to them that the three of them needed "marriage counseling" and that Matt would be able to help with that.

Roger confirmed the desire to resolve the conflict between him, Chris, and Neil. He also agreed with Chris and Neil that a better long-term solution was needed for the organizational structure. Matt spoke with Roger about the developmental needs of both Chris and Neil and agreed that a 360-feedback review for both Chris and Neil would be helpful. Matt suggested that the four of them – including Matt – meet after the 360 reviews were complete to address the conflict and the organizational structure. Roger also wanted Matt to work eventually with him and all of his direct reports, using the Enneagram to develop his leadership team.

With two weeks, the project shifted from coaching a high potential director to resolving a triangulated conflict, conducting two 360-feedback reviews, addressing an organizational structure issue, and training the CIO staff in using the Enneagram for leadership development. Chris and Neil were eager to get started. Roger said he was eager for everything to be running smoothly.

Chris and Neil had previously had a solid working relationship and both expressed a desire to have that again. The big change that happened in the system was when Roger was hired six months earlier. The question Matt asked himself was whether the role confusion and conflict was a natural result of the change or was there something else Roger was doing that was making the situation worse.

Roger agreed that Matt would interview fifteen different people from around the organization about Chris and Neil's leadership strengths and development areas, tabulate the results, and present each of them with their report. This would be the major data collection part of the project. No one else in the organization would see the report. Matt would also coach each of them every other week. After a couple of months of coaching, Matt would meet with Roger, Chris, and Neil to work through the organization structure issues and conflict. Training the CIO staff would come after that.

This triangulated system of Roger, Chris, and Neil seemed to be the real client; with Roger being the primary client. Other members of the CIO staff and CIO leadership team – the direct reports of the CIO staff – along with key internal IT customers were the other key people for both data collection and down the road for evaluation results.

In addition to being a certified coach, Matt also has extensive experience in conflict resolution, Enneagram in Business training, and many years of working in corporate environments. This project would grow into being the most complex he had ever contracted, but his skill set seemed to fit the situation, even though it would be a stretch.

The key success factors would be maintaining confidentiality of the coaching sessions with Chris and Neil and gaining and keeping their trust. Matt liked all three of the key players and took on the project because he could act in accordance with Roger's desire that all three of them have a successful future with the company.

Collecting

Data collection included individual interviews with Roger, Chris and Neil, plus fifteen other people at Silicon Valley Tech; internal IT customers and other key IT employees. The interview script was very open ended: *What does each person do well? What does he need to do to improve?* All interviewees' responses were recorded for each of the key clients: Roger, Chris and Neil. Once all data had been collected, the information was analyzed into common themes for each individual. Each person's report was about five pages long and included both positives and developmental areas.

In the course of the interviews, it became clear that many of the comments weren't directed at either Chris or Neil; the comments were general comments about the IT department. Matt decided to tabulate these comments about the IT department as a whole and give them to Roger in a separate report.

Communicating | data feedback

Matt emailed each person their respective reports two days prior to their next coaching session. This gave each of them the opportunity to read their report away from the office, have their initial reaction, sleep on it (aka "soak time"), and read it a time or two again prior to discussing the results with Matt.

By the time they had their individual coaching sessions, they were ready to discuss all of the findings objectively. Because one of them (Chris) was an Enneagram 1 and the other (Neil) an Enneagram 6, they both wanted to get right to the developmental areas as if they weren't able to read the positive comments the interviewees had made. Enneagram 1s want to make things right or correct problems quickly and effectively and Enneagram 6s worry that bad things will happen if problems are not resolved. Noting this dynamic, Matt took time with each of them to start first with a detailed review of the positive feedback that they had received. Then, Matt turned the discussion to their developmental topics.

As usual with 360-degree feedback assessments, the comments from others in the organization fit perfectly with their Enneagram types. Chris (type 1) was perceived as very thorough but at times lacking flexibility or interpersonal relatability. Neil (type 6) was considered to be a great problem solver who built loyalty within his team, but needed to develop a stronger "leadership presence" and pay more attention to managing the day-to-day operations. This feedback validated the Enneagram for both of these leaders, and solid developmental plans were built for each.

Before sharing the IT report with Roger, Matt let both Chris and Neil review it first and delete any comments they felt were directed at them (there were two such comments out of 150.) The IT issues had to do with being proactive versus reactive, the unclear role of IT, some miscalculations of cost IT had made in the previous months, and questions about IT's strategy. As with Chris and Neil, Matt shared the report with Roger a couple of days prior to meeting with him to discuss it. The meeting was less charged than with the other two because the report was 1) more generally about IT than specific to Roger, and 2) Roger had only been in place as CIO for less than a year and thus was still in his honeymoon period. Nevertheless, the report highlighted the suspicion that the organizational structure was confusing to everyone in the entire company. It was also clear that both Chris and Neil had solid professional reputations, but the perception was that each was being underutilized.

Challenging

At the conclusion of Matt's meeting with Roger, Matt was very direct: the data showed that the organizational structure issues needed remediation as soon as possible. Yes, IT needed work on its strategy. Yes, there was conflict between the three of them. But the most obvious issue to everyone internal and external to IT was the organizational structure. By solving it, the other two main issues – strategy and conflict – would be positively impacted. Strategy would take more time. Conflict would be difficult to separate from structure. Solve the structure first and then reassess. Roger was ready to take action. He agreed and set up a meeting with the four of them for the following week.

Changing | action planning and implementation

The meeting was in a small conference room. When Matt walked in, Chris was seated on the far side of the table; Roger was standing to the right at the whiteboard. Matt could either sit between Chris and Neil with Roger across the table from him, or sit next to Roger, across from Chris, with Neil on his left. Matt chose the former configuration for a number of reasons. First, he wanted to be as neutral as possible in the room, not to show any bias toward either Chris or Neil since they had competing interests. Second, he wanted to separate himself from Roger to balance the power dynamics in the room – Roger and Matt forming one polarity; Chris and Neil another. Had Matt chose to sit next to Roger, it would have reinforced the triangulation between the three of them as it would appear that Matt was just a part of Roger; by sitting across from Roger, the client triangle – at least for that meeting – became a diamond; shifting the client homeostasis.

Roger walked the team through Option A, which would split Chris' organization in half and give it to Neil to direct. Chris wasn't happy about this proposal because he would lose responsibility. However, with the organization growing as quickly as it was, it wouldn't be long before he was back at the same headcount, with more people working on fewer things. It wasn't clear if the organization could support Option A or not.

Option B was to create a new organization for Neil to manage that would leverage his problem solving abilities to be the system architect. This kind of role would be new to SVT, and it wasn't clear if the organization was large enough or ready enough for this kind of role. The agreement at the end of the meeting was to vet Option B with key stakeholders and reconvene in two weeks. All three of them seemed on board with the proposal.

Two weeks later, no follow up meeting had been scheduled. Chris seemed resigned to the fact that Option B wasn't going to happen. Neil expressed his doubts that it would ever work. He had spoken to a few key stakeholders who didn't give any support for the idea and encouraged against it. Neither had heard from Roger. Matt followed up with Roger, but no answer and no meeting scheduled.

In the meantime, the CIO Staff Enneagram training was scheduled and delivered. It was so successful the CIO leadership team received the same training two weeks later and, two weeks after that, some of their direct reports also received the training. At one of these trainings, Roger told Matt on a break that he had decided to go with Option A after all and was planning to tell Chris and Neil the following day. At lunch that day, the HR manager pulled Matt aside to ask thoughts on promoting Neil to Senior Director.

Option A was implemented along with a promotion for Neil. After the announcement, Chris and Matt had a deep coaching session in which Chris expressed a major change of career goals. He no longer felt a strong desire to become CIO any time soon. He was happy that the organization structure change had a very positive change on his working relationship with Neil. He was going to take this opportunity to work on his own leadership development.

At the next check in with Roger, he reported a noticeable improvement with both Chris and Neil as a result of the change and the ongoing coaching.

Closing | Assessment, institutionalization of the change, and separation

Everyone in the organization now considers the reorganization a success; the roles and responsibilities are clear, Neil and Chris are now peers and work together well, their teams are working well together where handoffs are needed, and the internal customers are getting good service.

The reorganization also dissolved the triangulation problem that was happening between Roger, Chris, and Neil, since Neil now reports directly to Roger. However, conflict still exists between Roger and Chris, just not about Neil. Neil is now experiencing similar conflict with Roger. Both Chris and Neil report that other members of the CIO staff are also having problems.

Coaching continues with Chris and Neil. Others on the CIO Staff and IT leadership team are requesting coaching. Additional Enneagram trainings have been delivered. Social intelligence is growing on the team. Last week the CIO left a voicemail for Matt. Noticing the normally bold CIO's voice was sheepish; Matt assumed it was the CIO calling to terminate services. No, in fact, it was the opposite; he was calling because he wanted coaching, too.

Conclusion

This is a classic case of "go as far as you can see and when you get there, you'll see farther." It started as an executive coaching project that met a specific need; both Chris and Neil benefited from the coaching. After that, "conflict resolution" was added to the project but, upon investigation, it became apparent that the organization structure was creating a lot of the conflict, so that was changed. But the underlying conflict was not addressed directly. Instead, an indirect approach was taken with the Enneagram leadership development training. In the second CIO staff session, Matt facilitated a discussion that enabled the team to go below the surface and express vulnerability in each other's presence. It was significant progress. Unfortunately, the CIO wasn't able to capitalize on that progress and instead engaged in some unskillful behavior towards his team over the next couple of weeks. But even that step back uncovered a deeper dynamic in the system, the CIO's own level of social intelligence. With that clarity, there is an opportunity for additional developmental work in this organization. Each person grows in his or her own time and own way, with assistance from the consultant.

Because he knew from the beginning of the project that Roger is an Enneagram 8, Matt turned up his energy level when interacting with Roger. This helped build rapport between Roger and Matt. In working with Chris and Neil, especially after learning about the conflict in the system, Matt was able to tap into his natural Enneagram

9 mediator strengths – Matt also has many years of conflict resolution work to lean on – and validate each person's point of view. Combined with his Enneagram knowledge, Matt was able to gain the trust and confidence of Chris and Neil early in their coaching relationships. Boundaries can be difficult for 9s if they aren't careful, so Matt made certain to establish with Roger that the two of them would not discuss the content of the coaching conversations Matt had with Chris and Neil. In a high growth company like Silicon Valley Tech, plans change quickly, often without much communication. Matt learned quickly that being flexible with schedule would be important. As a 9, the process of negotiating meeting times, dates, participant numbers, and agendas can be taxing for Matt; having to change all aspects of the plan at the last minute is downright distressing. By recognizing that the SVT culture still had a lot of adapt or die, start-up tech company paradigms, big, last-minute changes happen all the time, and to provide good service to the client, Matt was able to work within the system rather than against it.

Matt Ahrens is an organizational consultant, Enneagram teacher, and Senior Member of the Enneagram in Business Network. themattahrensgroup.com | matt@themattahrensgroup.com | (408) 230-9023

Case Studies | Social Intelligence Hiring
by Ginger Lapid-Bogda PhD

Context

Salesforce.com was going through a period of rapid expansion, including the creation of new sites away from its home base in San Francisco, California. Looking for cities where there was local talent and the quality of living would, therefore, be attractive to new hires or transfers, one location chosen was Portland, Oregon. But how were they going to find close to 200 top quality employees in a short 6-9 month time period, particularly in a city where there was keen competition for local talent?

Contracting

Todd, an Enneagram 7 leader with whom Ginger, an Enneagram 2, had worked with as a consultant at a prior organization, was fully familiar with her work and so sent her an email, asking if she could design and facilitate a one day hiring process. It would need to include the Enneagram, team behavior, and a team project in which candidates would be able to demonstrate their technical skills as well as their ability to function effectively on a self-organizing team.

Although Todd was the primary and initial client, he had designated a project manager, Pam, to handle the project oversight and logistics. In this sense, Ginger was now working with a client-pair, which added complexity to the project as it was designed and through the roll-out. In addition, the Salesforce culture is one in which input or feedback is freely given and often expected to be utilized, which also created more complexity and, at times, the need to recontract with both Todd and Pam in terms of who the client was as well as what feedback should and should not be integrated into the project.

Collecting

The data collection for this project was done primarily through Pam, the project manager, but in conjunction with Ginger in terms of the information needed to design and execute the project. In particular, data was collected from senior managers regarding how much time they would be willing to give to the one-day hiring process. Data from managers of all levels was also collected in terms of the criteria they were looking for in excellent candidates to hire. This data was then analyzed in terms of core requirements for the day-long event and the hiring criteria that needed to be met such that the day's activities would reveal, in action, the degree to which candidates met these criteria.

Communicating | data feedback

The data was analyzed and then communicated first to Pam, including the preliminary design for the day, particularly as the design satisfied both the project's purpose as defined by Todd and the data collected from managers. Design adjustments were made based on Pam's input, primarily in terms of paring down time and activities. The overall design can be seen below:

Social Intelligence Hiring (SIH) Process

For organizations that need to hire large numbers of great employees at all levels

6-step hiring process over a 3-month time period from start to finish

1. Recruit candidates (recruiters)
2. Meet potential candidates (managers and recruiters) at short social events to recommend candidates to feed into the Social Intelligence Hiring Day
3. Train candidate observers (managers, recruiters, and HR personnel) the day or evening prior to the actual SIH event
4. Conduct Social Intelligence Hiring Day (SIH)
5. Review all candidates (managers, recruiters, and HR personnel) and make decisions
6. Make job offers (recruiters) and give all candidates feedback (recruiters) within 48 hours

At Pam's strong urging, the candidate-hiring process had to begin at 8:30 am and end at 4:30 pm because the design included a 3-hour follow-up session where all participating managers, recruiters, and HR personnel would meet to review all candidates they had observed throughout the SIH day. This candidate review session was initially planned to occur the morning after the all-day candidate event, but Pam had been informed that many managers could not commit to this extra day, particularly when the SIH event occurred in a location where they did not live or work. In other words, they needed to fly home. As a result, the candidate review session was scheduled the actual evening of the SIH event, so the candidate assessment event (SIH) needed to end early or the assessors (managers, recruiters, and HR personnel) would be too tired to make optimal decisions. In order to end SIH at 4:30, some of the initial activities were eliminated and others shortened.

Once the above changes were made, Pam and Ginger conferred with Todd, who gave his final approval.

Challenging

The challenge came not from Pam or Todd, who fully understood and believed in the SIH approach and its core assumptions:

1. It's more important what candidates actually do as an on-the-job predictor of success, not what they say they have done or will do.
2. Any one manager or hiring person will have his or her own filter or bias*, but if multiple people are assessing the same individual, there will be less bias and even less bias when conversations about candidates occur through open dialogue with others.
3. A candidate may be an excellent interviewer but not work well with peers.
4. It's hard for a candidate to be fake or be someone they are not for a whole day, but this is possible to do in a one-hour interview.

5. Social and Emotional Intelligence matter as much or more than actual hard skills, as hard skills can be easily taught, although some more easily than others.
6. The ability to handle change and stress in a resourceful way – and particularly in a team context – is crucial to success at work, at least at Salesforce.

*bias refers to many factors, such as hiring someone you perceive as similar to yourself; reading into a person's background or resume and assuming the candidate has certain skill sets; hiring people you like or would want to have as a social friend; and/or not responding positively to individuals based on age, race, gender, sexual orientation or some other factor.

Interestingly but not really a surprise, the challenges came at the evening training for the assessors, who would be observing candidates throughout the following day. Although they agreed with most of the above assumptions, the idea of trusting another assessor's observations of a candidate for a position for which they were responsible was non-traditional and a big stretch. Even though it made clear that the "hiring manger" had ultimate hiring decision-making authority for a given candidate, the idea of really taking input from others was a big stretch. At first, we had to reassure them and invite them to experiment with the new hiring process. After the first SIH, we were able to rely on managers who had already been through the process who could offer testimonials and examples of candidates they might have hired, but who would have been a wrong hire were it not for information gleaned from other assessors.

Changing | action planning and implementation

Social Intelligence Hiring (SIH) Process
The Social Intelligence Hiring Process is shown in two graphics, one that compares SIH with traditional hiring and the other that illustrates the entire SIH process from start to finish *(see pages 156-157)*.

In SIH, the Enneagram was used, not to hire by type because Enneagram type does not correlate to hard or soft skills. The Enneagram was used to assess the degree of self-awareness of each candidate, as well as the candidate's commitment to self-development, whether this be via the Enneagram or some other approach. Candidate team-based behavior was assessed twice, first by observing them during a playful and challenging team activity and, second, through their behavior on project teams during which each team was given a business-related project topic for which they had to develop a solution and then present this to a panel of Salesforce personnel. Just as important as the candidates' behavior during the above activities was how candidates engaged with Salesforce staff of various levels and how they interacted with other candidates. For example, a candidate might be solicitous with hiring managers but rude to support staff, or a candidate might demonstrate strong social skills with Salesforce personnel, but act overly competitive or dismissive with other candidates. All of this information gathered was fed into the evening candidate review session.

Compare Innovative SIH with Traditional Hiring

Hiring Factors	Innovative Social Intelligence Hiring	Traditional Hiring
Hiring focus	Team players Candidate in context Whole person Culture creators Present and future aptitude	Individuals Candidate out of context Job description fit Current culture alignment Past and present skills
Hiring based on	Self-mastery skills Interpersonal effectiveness Influencing ability Reasoning skills Engagement Passion Resilience Initiative Innovation Applied technical knowledge	Technical skills Interviewing skills
Hiring methodology	Real-time observation Multiple raters (15+) Competence in action	Interviewing Single raters Self-reported competence
Risk of wrong hires	Low	Moderate to high
Hiring time	1 day event *3-4 months from sourcing to hiring*	Multiple interviews; multiple months *7-8 months from sourcing to hiring*
Decision maker	Hiring manager with abundant real-time input from multiple assessors and perspectives	Hiring manager with or without lag-time input from a few others
Candidate experience	Transparent Exciting Builds networks and skills Receive quick and precise feedback	Opaque Tedious Isolating Wait for extended time with minimal or no feedback
Hiring personnel experience	Engaging Educates re effective team behavior, self mastery, and influencing skills Enhances organizational team work	Monotonous No secondary learning No organizational side-benefits
Useful for	Start-ups Multiple hires needed in either one area or a variety of functions	One-off hires

Social Intelligence Hiring

Hire large numbers of best-in-class employees who are immediately up-and-running

Recruit candidates

Candidate Pool

Direct inquiries

Employee referrals

Networks | personal | professional

Social media in f g

News organizations

Professional associations

Assess technical competency
Where relevant, check candidate technical competency

Meet candidates
Invite candidates to social events for initial in-person screening

Train assessors

Invite to event
Invite viable candidates to Social Intelligence Hiring Day

Social Intelligence Day
A full day of great activities where you get to see your potential hires as they truly are as human beings, team members, and innovators

Review & choose
All assessors review and discuss all candidates

Feedback given to all candidates

Offers

Here are the results of SIH, which Salesforce first used in recruiting candidates for the Portland office and then used, because it was so successful, with their hiring in the IT function within San Francisco.

FASTER RECRUITING
Reduces time from source to hire from 7-8 months to 3-4 months
Large numbers of candidates are hired at the same time

BETTER HIRES
Excellent candidate yield: every Social Intelligence Hiring has generated, on average, a 25% yield; thus, with 48 potential, prequalified candidates, 12 get hired (using an absolute standard for hiring, not a relative one so no quality compromises are made)
Eliminates wrong hires: candidates hired based on what they can do and strong social intelligence rather than on what they say they can do or those with poor team and interpersonal skills
Identifies "sleeping stars" as well as "rock stars": enables organization to see gifts and strengths of non-flashy candidates
Quick onboarding: SIH experience familiarizes candidates with the company culture and personnel
Accelerated productivity: new hires integrate quickly and easily into existing or new teams

LOWER COST PER HIRE
Reduced recruiter time: recruiters need fewer contacts with candidates and managers regarding candidates
Reduced manager time: managers observe and interact with many candidates in one day rather than having to engage in extended interviews with individual candidates over many months

Closing | assessment, institutionalization of the change, and separation

Todd was thrilled with the result. It was his vision materialized plus more. As a 7, Todd dreams big, and this became bigger than he first imagined. The SIH process was so dynamic, exciting, and productive, that after the first few events, Todd no longer needed to even attend.

As a 2, Ginger was enthused with the result, although the path along the way was, at times, rocky. Almost every time a SIH was to take place, feedback was given by managers, often only as individuals rather than as part of a group consensus, to change some aspect of the process. As a 2, she was caught between wanting very much to satisfy customer requests and her belief that some of these suggestions were process changes rather than process improvements. Some ideas, on the other hand, did improve the process. And still other ideas would take SIH in an entirely different direction from what was intended. Sorting this out became a challenge in terms of when to make the changes and when to push back and say this will not have the desired impact. That said, it was a small price to pay for such an innovative way of hiring.

There were other positive impacts of SIH that were not intended, but were nonetheless exiting for both Todd and Ginger. First, the managers who became involved in SIH, and eventually it included almost all managers, began to function as a strong and cohesive team across 4-5 levels of management. Many of them worked in different locations, even in different cities, and many had never met one another. The managers also became proficient in the Enneagram and brought it into their own teams because they saw how much value the Enneagram brought to being more emotionally and socially intelligent. In addition, managers observed in real time what contributed to and what impaired teams from being highly effective and productive from observing so many different teams functioning during SIH. Managers also brought this back to their own teams and this increased their ability to be even better team leaders.

Candidates also benefited, whether or not they were hired. Pam was adamant about candidates having the best experience possible. Most candidates said they actually forgot, as the day went on, that they were part of a hiring process, experiencing it more as a free training day. Candidates who were hired felt they already knew senior management and middle management, something that would not have occurred in the traditional hiring process. In addition, SIH was like a "boot camp" for new hires so that they felt on-boarded before they began. Thus, orienting candidates who had been hired through SIH became a faster and easier process.

Conclusion

These conclusions are taken from the Deloitte Review, Issue 13, 2013 (p. 16); Deloitte studied the process from beginning to end.

"Brand-conscious companies that treat the candidate with the same attention and focus that they give their customers should find the Social Intelligence Hiring model to be impactful. In implementing this model, several guidelines have emerged as especially helpful:

Focus on more than just technical skills by having the candidate participate in a variety of activities that reveal his or her personality, creativity, emotional maturity, and social intelligence.

Design the recruiting process to mirror how work actually gets done within the company; emphasize team activities for companies that have team-based cultures.

Use extended workshops rather than a short series of interviews as the interaction will more accurately reveal who a candidate is in different contexts.

Drive and nurture connectivity, collaboration, and sustained relationships between candidates and with the company through social media tools.

Demonstrate to the candidate the importance that the company places on potential employees by actively involving and providing access to senior management who are committed to be at the workshop events.

Build trusted relationships by being transparent with the candidates and letting them know that the process is about helping them succeed so that they understand and appreciate what you are doing and how it helps them become better."

CHAPTER 11
ACTIVITIES | CONSULTING with THE ENNEAGRAM

Tell me and I'll forget; show me and I may remember; involve me and I'll understand.
Chinese proverb

Consultants need to be creative, using proven activities and
change interventions with skill and grace, but also being
able to generate new activities and technologies suited to
particular client needs. Here are some great activities that are
focused on specific topics, experiential, and quite powerful:

Bingo warm-up

Team simulation

Team interdependence

Diversity

Visioning

Strategy

Bingo Warm-Up Activity

Objective | To generate energy, get people to know each other in a short period of time, and to communicate elements of organizational culture

Audience | 25 people minimum to very large groups; best done with people who don't know each other well

Time | 15-30 minutes, depending on group size

Materials | Bingo cards (customized for the organization) and instead of numbers, use 20 categories related to work and personal life; 3 prizes (can be 3 of the same item or 3 different items)

PREPARATION

Explain the purpose: to meet as many people as possible through finding out who has affirmative responses to the items in each Bingo square, then getting that person to sign the Bingo card.

Explain the following rules: Get one signature in each box (there are 20 boxes) | People can only sign two boxes per Bingo card (but can sign multiple Bingo cards) | The person whose name is in the box must be the person who signs the card | All answers must be truthful | First 3 winners bring completed Bingo cards to designated person to claim prizes.

ACTIVITY

Hand out bingo cards, have participants stand up and move to a central part of the room where there is space to mingle. Ask if they have any questions (before the activity starts), and answer all questions that you can.

Start the activity, joining in with the participants to make sure the activity and interactions are going well. You can also sign Bingo cards if you like. Just make sure if you do, there is a 2nd person who can stand near the front of the room to take cards from the first 3 winners.

The winners (first 3 people) should have their cards verified to make sure that all boxes have a signature written in them and that no one has signed the same card more than once. If any of the first 3 "winners" do not meet the criteria, then verify person 4 and/or 5.

Once you have 3 winners, stop all activity, announce the winners in the order they finished the activity, and hand out the prizes.

Enneagram Team Simulation Activity

Objective | To give people the experience of being in real time and to examine their individual team behavior as well as team processes

Audience | Minimum of 7 people; maximum of 12

Time | 45 minutes or longer

Materials | Large plastic bag filled with soft balls of all sizes and texture

---

PREPARATION

Form 7-10 participants into a circle, all standing, facing each other; if possible, have all Enneagram styles represented; if more than 10 participants, have others observe.

Explain that you are the CEO of an organization, whose job it is to pass balls to other team members without dropping them. There are several rules that must be followed:

  Balls can't be handed to the person on either side of you
  All dropped balls must be picked up and put back in circulation
  Everyone can stand no closer than their starting position, but they can stand further apart
  There is no talking of any kind once play has started

Ask if they have any questions before play starts; answer all questions that you can.

PLAY

Start play, going around the outside of the circle and giving different kinds of balls to different players, but not all at once; keep adding balls as the team seems to be able to handle more and more (this usually goes on for about 10 minutes or so).

Stop the play and ask the ball group (each person) these questions (one set of questions answered by all players, then go to the next questions):

  How did it go? How does your perception of how it went reflect your Enneagram style?
  How did you experience your Enneagram style in action (both what you did during play and what was going on within you)?
  What did you notice about the team's interactions, processes, and success? How does this reflect the Enneagram styles in this group?
  If you had a chance to do it again, what would you change, if anything, and what would you keep?

DEBRIEFING OPTIONS

Have them do the activity again, then use the same process questions as above as a chance for process improvements.

Ask the observers what they noticed in terms of Enneagram styles in action. Then do the simulation again.

If you have at least 6 people of the same type, you can have them do the activity, then process team work styled of that type.

Team Interdependence Activity

Objective | To highlight team interdependencies

Audience | Teams of up to 40 people

Time | 1 hour or longer, depending on team size

Materials | Heavy popsicle sticks or long pencils (unsharpened); ample ball of string or strong yarn that can be easily thrown across a room and won't break (use 2 different colors); Training Tool: Goals and Interdependence

Note | Make sure that this is a real team – that they have at least 1 common goal and some degree of interdependence

---

PREPARATION

Explain the idea of team interdependence, giving sports examples of high, medium, and low interdependence teams (basketball, football, golf, respectively). Describe Enneagram style preferences for levels of interdependence and the importance of focusing on what is optimal for the team task, taking individual preferences into account but not designing interdependence around these style preferences.

Ask participants to stand in a circle and give each person one popsicle stick or long pencil.

Explain that they are going to clarify their interdependencies using these instructions: One person gets the ball of string, wraps the loose end around his or her pencil or stick and selects someone in the group on who the 1st person is interdependent. The first person throws the yarn to the person, saying his or her name and articulating the interdependency. That person then wraps the string around his or her pencil or stick and selects someone in the group and continues the same process.

ACTIVITY

Use 1 color ball to begin and give this to 1 person in the group, have him or her wind the end of the yarn around the stick, then throw it to another team member while verbally stating the interdependency ("I am interdependent with _____ because _____").

Ask the person to who the ball was thrown to do the same thing: wrap the ball around his or her stick, then throw the ball to another team member while verbally stating the interdependency using the same sentence as above.

Keep the activity going until they have articulated most of the current interdependencies.

Ask them to keep holding their string and sticks and to look at the "web" they have created. Then solicit comments from team members about what they notice. Pay particular attention to team members who either (a) have a large number of strings; (b) individuals who have very few strings; and (c) other obvious configurations such as groups of people who are clearly strong together. Ask about the meaning of these patterns.

Finally, ask if their current "web" of interdependencies is optimal or if there is something that would be helpful to change, and facilitate that discussion.

ADDITIONAL OPTIONS

If the team needs more interdependencies to be effective, use the 2nd ball of string (a different color from the 1st ball), and ask them to do the same activity, overlaying the 2nd "web" on the 1st).

If the team needs fewer interdependencies to be effective, use the 2nd ball of string (a different color from the 1st ball), and ask them to do the same activity, but put the old "web" on the floor and use new sticks with the new yarn.

This activity can be used when a team is ending, as a ritual of closure with people expressing appreciations rather than interdependencies.

Diversity Activity

Objective | To help participants understand the multiple aspects of our differences, how these impact us, and how the Enneagram impacts our different identities

Audience | No minimum or maximum

Time | 1 hour or longer

Materials | Graphic of the Diversity Circle

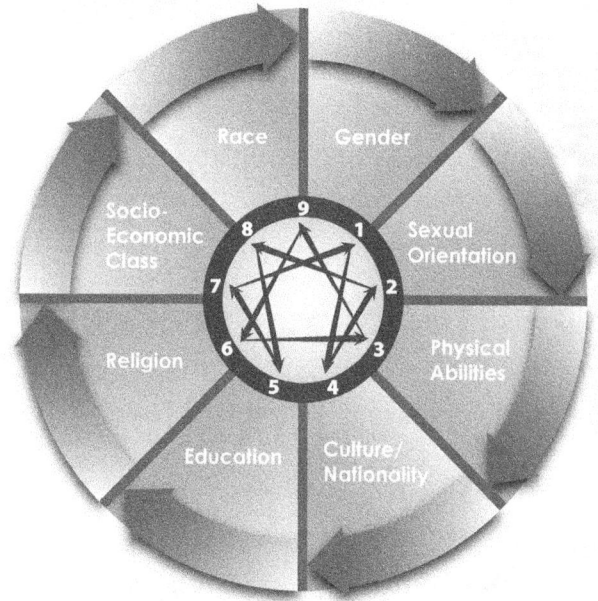

PREPARATION

Explain the concept of Diversity in terms of (a) how people define themselves; (b) how they are defined by others; (c) their social referent groups and how much they identify with them; (d) informal or formal bias, and discrimination; and (e) power differences.

Explain what is meant by each of the dimensions of Diversity on the circle. In addition, explain that other factors may also be important Diversity factors for some people – for example, age, tribal group, being raised in a supportive family setting, etc.

Explain how the Enneagram permeates each of these dimensions of Diversity and also how a person's Enneagram style can be a key element on the Diversity Circle – for example, how people of certain types may be treated differently based on national, ethnic culture or even company culture.

ACTIVITY

Warm-up

Discuss which aspects of the Diversity Circle most impact you personally in terms of your social identity, and which aspects impact you the least. This can be done in pairs, small heterogeneous groups, racial or gender groups, type groups, etc. Facilitate a very short report if done in groups rather than pairs.

Power, Rank, and Privilege Continuum | Explanation

Explain the following: Each Diversity dimension also comes with varying degrees of rank or privilege. Often when the rank or privilege is higher, we are not as aware of this as when we are when the rank or privilege is lower. How is rank or privilege determined? Often the level of privilege is socially determined or constructed and then enforced or reinforced through social institutions – organizations, laws, the media – but also through social norms, interactions, and mental models held by individuals and groups.

Power, Rank, and Privilege Continuum | Activity

Place a long straight line of white tape at the end of the room so all participants can stand behind it with some room behind them. Tell them that you are going to name one dimension of Diversity at a time, and they will be asked whether on this dimension, they believe they themselves have power, rank, or privilege. If yes, they move one step forward. If no, they move one step backward. If neither yes nor no, they stay where they are. Start first with race, and ask if their race gives them power, privilege, or rank. If yes, take a step forward. If no, step backward one step. If neutral, stay where they are. Ask them to look around to see who is standing where. Then say the second dimension: gender. Follow the same process. Do this until you cover all the categories in the Diversity circle. Finally, add age and then coming from a nurturing and supportive family background.

Power, Rank, and Privilege Continuum | Debriefing of people at similar levels

Ask participants to go into groups of 3-4 with people on a similar ending place on the floor (this groups people into similar levels of Diversity-based power), and ask them to discuss the following: (a) why did you place yourself where you did on each dimension; (b) what is your experience having the level of power, rank, and privilege that you do; (c) what surprised you; and (d) how does your Enneagram style factor into these various dimensions as well as your privilege that comes from that style?

Power, Rank, and Privilege Continuum | Debriefing of people at different levels

Ask participants to go into groups of 3-4 with people on a different ending place on the floor, and ask them to discuss the following: (a) how your experience was different from others; and (b) what is the impact of being at these very different levels for you and people similar to you? Do brief reports from small groups, going from most powerful to least.

Visioning Activity

Objective | To develop a shared, compelling organizational vision

Audience | Any size team

Time | 1 hour or more, depending on group size

Materials | Paper and pencils; flip charts; magic markers

PREPARATION

Tell participants they will be doing a visioning exercise by imagining in their minds what the organization will be like in X number of years (client selects 1 year, 3 years or 5 years, depending on the group needs).

As a sample, ask each person to relax, then imagine they are on their favorite vacation. *Where are they? What is their environment like? Who are they with? What are they doing?*

Debrief this short activity, asking a few people to share where they went and what it was like. Reinforce that they can all do the next exercise given that they could do this one — imagining where they would be on a vacation.

ACTIVITY

Tell them they are going to imagine the organization X years from now, and you will guide them with suggestions for what to think about. Suggest that if you move to another topic, they should continue their own imaginings and then rejoin you when they are ready. They can write down ideas as they come, but you will also give them time at the end to do this.

Ask them to relax and to imagine it is X years from now and you are all celebrating the success of _____ (organization's name). _____ (organization's name) has been successful beyond what it had thought possible. Where are you? Who else is there? What is the environment like – visually, sounds, smells, general atmosphere. Give them time to settle into their images before you move on (about 45 seconds to 1 minute).

Ask them a series of questions that make sense to you, allowing about 45 second intervals between questions. These should be adjusted to the group. Here are samples in somewhat of a sequence:

[Name the key leader] is there, stands up, and makes comments to everyone about the organization's success. What does he or she say we have done so well and its contribution to the entire organization?

[Name a secondary person] gets the opportunity to thank everyone for what we have accomplished. What do they say? What is highlighted in terms of programs and extraordinary efforts?

Several people are called up for special recognition. You are called up and given an award. What is the award for, and what was your special contribution?

Who else is called up, and what is said about them?

[Name the leader] talks about the values that were underneath our efforts and what drove our action. What core values are talked about?

A reporter from (name a key radio or TV station or a newspaper) wants to interview you about the success of your team's efforts. The reporter asks you what you think created this success, what were the biggest obstacles that had to be overcome, and how did you overcome them.

Imagine you are leaving the event and meeting with someone significant to you – a spouse, close friend, child, or relative. This person says, "You seem so proud of this effort. What are you most proud of?"

Give people about 2 minutes to finish their visioning.
Ask them to jot down their thoughts on paper (5-10 minutes).
Ask them to share their visions, one person at a time (not reading from the sheet). Allow time for this, and do not rush it.

Ask, "What did you hear in common, and what did you hear that really excited you, even if only one person said it?"
Chart the common ideas; also chart ideas they find compelling, even if these were not common.

Ask people what they experienced during the visioning exercise, both their individual visioning as well as hearing those of others. Ask for 3 volunteers to take the experience and chart paper and then draft a simple, compelling vision statement from it to bring back to the group later for reflection and refinement.

Mission | Strategy Activity

Objective | To develop an organizational, business unit, or large team strategy

Audience | Any size team

Time | 1.5 to 2 days

Materials | Multiple flip charts with extra pads; various colored magic markers

Note | The group/team with which you are working would either need to have a viable vision currently or you would need to do the visioning activity with them prior to this activity

---

PREPARATION

Introduce Concepts

Show and explain the strategic planning graphic.

Review the *strategic planning* grid that shows each element of the strategic process. Make sure to review the Gandhi example.

ACTIVITY

Start play, going around the outside of the circle and giving different kinds of balls to different players, but not all at once; keep adding balls as the team seems to be able to handle more and more (this usually goes on for about 10 minutes or so).

Mission Development

Divide participants into small groups, each with a flip chart and magic markers. Ask them to create their best idea of the mission statement that aligns with their vision, one that indicates what business they are in. (20 minutes)

Have each group put their draft on a chart pad and share with the other groups. Place each easel side by side with no comments from the group.

Ask them what all groups had in common and which ones they found most compelling.

Ask for a group of volunteers, one from each group, to go off-line and redo the mission statement.

Call a break.

After the break, review the work of the volunteers, and ask for input.

Either rework the statement with the whole group or ask the volunteers to go off again and try to redo the statement. Make sure all work is on chart pads.

After two iterations, the mission statement is usually close enough to begin the strategy section.

Strategy Development

Re-explain strategy. Divide them into new groups, making sure the groups are diverse by function, knowledge, etc., and ask them to consider this question: If you were limited to 3 (not more than 5) approaches (not activities) to achieving your mission and vision, what would that be? Have the small groups develop their best thoughts. Make sure to visit each group to make sure they are at the strategic and not tactical level. Repeat the process above.

Goal Development

Re-explain goals (measurable outcomes) and link them to the Balanced Scorecard. Divide people into groups based on the strategy areas they know most about – one strategy per group. Have them develop no more than 5 goals for their strategy (with measures) and follow the same process as above.

When the groups are satisfied with all their goals, have them examine their goals against the strategy by asking this question: *If you could accomplish all these goals, would your strategy be successful? If not, what do you need to change?*

Tactic Development

Repeat the same process as for goal development (keeping people in the same groups).

Closure

Review the entire work (from vision, mission, all the way to tactics) to make certain they are all aligned and support the mission and vision. They assign responsibilities for the goals and/or tactical areas.

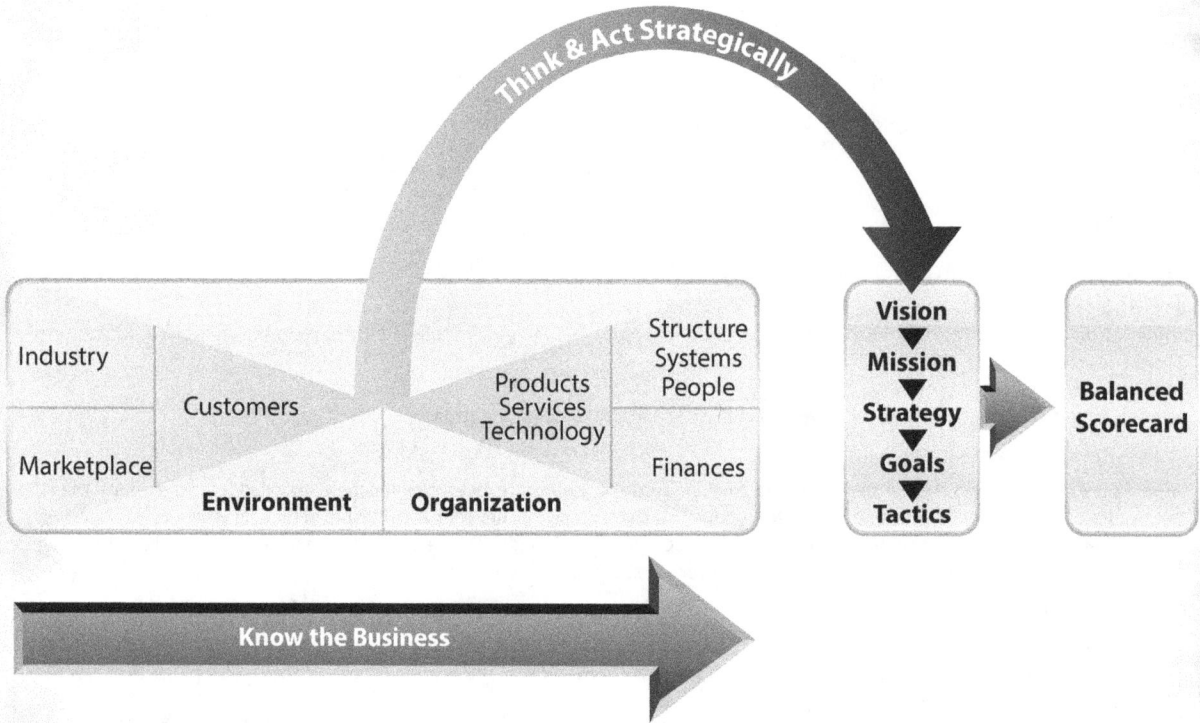

Think and Act Strategically

STRATEGIC ELEMENT	DEFINITION	POTENTIAL PITFALLS	EXAMPLE: GANDHI
VISION	**A shared, compelling, and enduring picture or understanding of the preferred future** The vision endures for a number of years (3 to 5 or longer) and is the first strategic element to be developed.	Too lofty, too complex, not compelling; not values based; not grounded in reality; undercommunicated; underutilized	Create a free, independent and spiritual state of India, with full citizenship and dignity conferred on all its people
MISSION	**The concrete business you are in; your business charter; the value you add to your customers that enables you to achieve your vision** The mission supports the vision and represents your special and specific contribution to the vision; it remains steady and changes only if the environment changes significantly.	Too many or too few lines of business; unclear customers or limited value to customers; thinking your product is your mission	Have people from India in control of the Indian government; integrate Hindus and Muslims into a common country
STRATEGY	**The approaches you will take in order to accomplish your mission and vision; strategy determines resource allocations and other critical decisions** Strategies contain an action orientation and usually consist of 3 to 5 strategies that will accomplish your mission; these are usually changed only after changing tactics and/or goals have proved ineffective.	Confusion of tactics with strategies; no strategy, too many or too few strategies; strategies not comprehensive, linked, or leveraged; strategies vague or nonactionable	Peaceful, targeted, and nonviolent large scale civil disobedience; no economic dependence on any outside country
GOALS	**Measurable goals that represent key outcomes and milestones for the strategies** There are usually 3 to 5 goals per strategy, although some goals can be leveraged and used for more than one strategy; goals are changed only if trying alternative tactics proves ineffective.	Too many or too few goals; insufficient commitment to them; goals not linked directly to strategies; goals not measurable, not clear, or not differentiated enough from each other	Independence granted; minimal incidents of violence (prefer no violence whatsoever)
TACTICS	**Specific actions to accomplish each goal** There are usually 3 to 5 tactics per goal, although some tactics can be leveraged and used for more than one goal; tactics can be readily changed if they are not achieving the goals, strategy, and mission.	Ineffective tactics; insufficient resources for implementation; responsibility not assigned	Vast numbers of people going to jail in protest; salt rebellion (making own salt rather than buying it from England); making own cloth rather than being dependent on England for textiles

APPENDIX | CONSULTING with THE ENNEAGRAM

Wings, Arrows and Subtypes

People often ask why individuals of the same Enneagram type may appear quite different from one another. Although your type remains the same throughout your lifetime, some aspects of your type may soften and also transform into strengths rather than limitations as you grow and develop. There are also overlays that may occur with certain individuals – for example, overlays of culture, gender, and even those of other dominant family members. The answer can also be found in the Enneagram system itself. In addition to these subtle differences that influence how your Enneagram type manifests – though these do not change the basic architecture of your personality character – there are also three different Enneagram-based elements that influence your thinking, feeling, and behavior: wings, arrow lines, and Enneagram subtypes.

Enneagram Wings

Wings are the Enneagram types on each side of your actual Enneagram type. These are secondary types of your core personality type, which means that you may also display some of the characteristics of these Enneagram types. Wings do not fundamentally change your Enneagram type; they merely add additional qualities to your core personality. As can be seen on the Enneagram symbol, Nine and Two are wings for Ones, One and Three are wings for Twos, Two and Four are wings for Threes, and so forth.

You may have one wing, two wings, or no wings at all. It is also common to have had one wing be more active when you were younger, and to have had another appear as you matured. People of the same Enneagram type and identical wings may use their wing qualities differently. However, the general wing descriptions for all nine Enneagram types given here may serve as guidelines to help you explore this aspect of the Enneagram and also help you to identify your wing or wings.

Enneagram Arrows

Arrow lines refer to the two types on the Enneagram symbol that have arrows pointing away from or toward your core Enneagram type, and you may show some characteristics of one or both of these two additional types. Access to your arrow lines can be beneficial to you, adding complexity, nuance, and flexibility to your personality, but they do not change your fundamental type – that is, your patterns of thinking and feeling and motivational structure remain the same. You may have strong links to one arrow number, both arrow numbers, or neither arrow number. People of the same Enneagram type who have strong links to their arrow numbers may use these arrow qualities quite differently.

Enneagram Subtypes

Enneagram subtypes are a third element that may affect your personality character structure. Subtypes are the way in which the particular emotional pattern for each Enneagram type most frequently manifests in that person's behavior. There are three different subtypes for each Enneagram type: self-preservation subtypes of all nine types manifest their type through a particular behavior related to issues of self-preservation; social subtypes of all nine types focus primarily on social issues, often behavior in response to social groups; one-to-one subtypes of all nine types are more oriented to one-to-one relationships. More specifically, self-preservation refers to issues of physical existence, safety, security, danger, resources, and structure/control; social refers to belonging, community, groups, social relationships, and influence; and one-to-one refers to oneself in relation to one other person, affection, intimacy, bonding, attraction, and one-to-one relationships. To have one of these instincts more active in us does not necessarily mean we are good at it, like it, or are satisfied in this arena. It means our attention and energy goes most consistently either toward that area, away from it, or that we have the most ambivalence in that arena.

Wings, Arrows and Subtypes | Enneagram Ones

Wings for Ones
Nine Wing: Ones with a Nine wing have a greater ability to relax and unwind without having to go on vacation, are less reactive when they disagree with someone, and are more likely to solicit the opinions of others rather than relying primarily on their own judgments or those of others whom they respect.

Two Wing: Ones with a Two wing are more consistently generous and people-focused, in addition to being more gregarious and displaying more consistent warmth to others.

Arrow Lines for Ones
Arrow Line to Four: Ones who have a strong connection to type Four pay more attention to their own inner experiences and are therefore more introspective and aware of their own feelings. In addition, a link to Four adds originality and creativity to the ways in which Ones approach work, life, and any aesthetic interests they may have.

Arrow Line from Seven: Ones who have a strong connection to Seven are far more flexible, spontaneous, innovative, and lighthearted, and they have more fun.

Three Subtypes for Ones
Although all Ones seek perfection and avoid mistakes and experience anger as chronic dissatisfaction and irritation with the many things in life and work that are not as they should be, there are three distinct ways in which Ones manifest these characteristics.

Self-Preservation Subtype Ones focus on getting everything structured and organized correctly and experience anxiety, worry, and irritation when they think this may not occur. Wanting to make sure that everything is under control, they emphasize precision and extreme accuracy as a way to make certain that everything is done right.

Social Subtype Ones perceive themselves as role models who represent the right way of being and behaving. In their view, they set the standard for their particular reference groups. Teaching by example, social subtype Ones also focus their efforts on social institutions, often critiquing them as a way to perfect them.

One-to-One Subtype Ones have a driving need to perfect others, particularly those who matter to them, as well as to perfect society in general. They perceive reforming others as both their right and their responsibility, and they go about this with intensity and passion.

Wings, Arrows and Subtypes | Enneagram Twos

Wings for Twos

One Wing: When Twos have access to their One wing, they balance their focus on people with a dedication to task, are more discerning about situations and people, pay more attention to detail, and have an increased ability to be firm and to say no, with far less worry about how others will react to them when they assert themselves in this way.

Three Wing: Twos with a Three wing are far more comfortable being visible, such as holding a high-profile leadership position. In addition, these Twos feel more comfortable acknowledging their desire to be successful; in fact, they often pursue being respected as much as being liked.

Arrow Lines for Twos

Arrow Line to Eight: Twos with a strong link to Eight have a far deeper sense of their own personal power, tend to be bolder and more candid, and are more in touch with their energy and the power of their anger.

Arrow Line from Four: Twos who are strongly connected to Enneagram type Four have increased emotional depth, because they focus on their own emotional reactions as much as on the feelings of others. They also tend to be more creative and original.

Three Subtypes for Twos

All Twos have their sense of self-worth, personal pride, and importance integrally linked with how others respond to them and want to be viewed as appealing individuals who are valued for helping others and for being able to influence things in a positive direction. There are three distinct ways in which Twos manifest these characteristics.

Self-Preservation Subtype Twos deny their own needs for protection while at the same time trying to attract others who will provide exactly that for them. Drawing others to them in the same way that children do – that is, by being appealing and appearing to be without guile – self-preservation Twos are also ambivalent about close relationships and less trusting than social subtype or one-to-one subtype Twos.

Social Subtype Twos focus on helping groups more than individuals and are more intellectually oriented and comfortable being in visibly powerful positions than individuals of the other two subtype variations. Social subtype Twos are less concerned with how specific individuals respond to them and more focused on group-level reactions, which is a result of their desire to stand above the crowd in some way.

One-to-One Subtype Twos are primarily oriented to individual relationships and meeting the needs of important people and partners. They try to attract specific individuals as a way of getting their needs met – that is, they feel they have value when chosen by someone important – but they are also highly motivated to meet the needs of these individuals as a way of developing and sustaining the relationship.

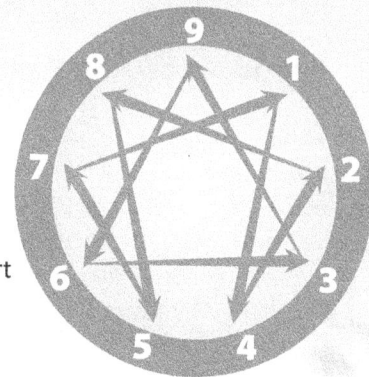

Wings, Arrows and Subtypes | Enneagram Threes

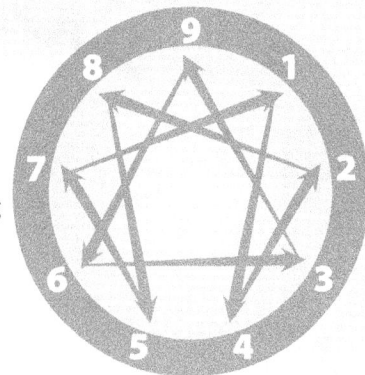

Wings for Threes

Two Wing: Threes with Two wings are far more sensitive to the feelings of others and more generous with their time and resources, and they often focus on helping others in their professional and/or personal lives.

Four Wing: Threes who have a Four wing are far more in contact with their own feelings, are willing to engage in emotional conversations with others, have a deeper personal presence, and may engage in some form of artistic expression or refined level of artistic appreciation.

Arrow Lines for Threes

Arrow Line to Nine: When Threes have a strong connection to arrow line Nine, they use this to relax, slow down their pace, and engage in activities simply for the pleasure of doing them. Being able to access type Nine also helps Threes to be more mellow and easygoing.

Arrow Line from Six: Although many Threes are smart, accessing their arrow line Six augments their normal intelligence with an enhanced analytical capability and insightfulness. In addition, Threes with a link to type Six tend to be more aware of their own true reactions rather than engaging in work as a way to avoid their feelings.

Three Subtypes for Threes

All Threes feel they must appear successful in order to gain the admiration and respect of others, and they avoid failure in any form by hiding parts of themselves that do not conform to their image of success, deceiving not only others, but also themselves as they come to believe that the image they create is actually who they are. There are three distinct ways in which Threes manifest these characteristics.

Self-Preservation Subtype Threes try to be seen as self-reliant, autonomous, and hardworking, thus portraying an image of being a good or ideal person. The self-preservation Three may even create an image of having no image.

Social Subtype Threes want to be seen as successful and admirable in the context of specific reference groups – that is, the groups in which they want to be seen as successful. They like to be around other successful people, because this proximity reinforces both the Three's image and status.

One-to-One Subtype Threes want to be viewed as successful by people who are very important to them, partly by appearing attractive to these people in some way but also by helping them to achieve success.

Wings, Arrows and Subtypes | Enneagram Fours

Wings for Fours

Three Wing: When Fours have a Three wing, they are more action oriented, have higher and more consistent energy levels, exhibit more poise and confidence, and are more comfortable with being highly visible rather than shying away from visibility or feeling ambivalent about it.

Five Wing: Fours with a Five wing are more objective and analytical, which provides a counterpoint to their more subjective emotional way of relating with others. In addition, they have an increased ability to perceive situations from a more considered and less reactive perspective and often demonstrate more self-restraint and self-containment.

Arrow Lines for Fours

Arrow Line to Two: Because Fours normally focus on their own internal responses and personal experiences, a strong link to their arrow line Two greatly enhances their attunement to other people. This increased attention to others helps these Fours be more responsive and more consistent in their interactions.

Arrow Line from One: When Fours have a strong connection to their arrow line One, they become more objective and discerning of people and events rather than making assessments based primarily on their emotional reactions. This provides them with greater balance, increased emotional and mental clarity, and enhanced attention to details.

Three Subtypes for Fours

All Fours desire a feeling of deep connection both with their own interior worlds and with other people as a way to avoid feeling deficient or not good enough. Because they believe there is something lacking within them – although they cannot define exactly what this is – Fours consciously and unconsciously compare themselves to others (referred to as envy) as a way to determine what is wrong, consequently feeling superior, deficient, or both. There are three distinct ways in which Fours manifest these characteristics.

Self-Preservation Subtype Fours try to bear their suffering in silence as a way to prove that they are good enough by virtue of enduring inner anguish. In addition, they engage in nonstop activity and/or reckless behavior as a way to feel excited and energized and to avoid not feeling as good as others. Of all three subtypes, self-preservation Fours do not appear to be as envious or sensitive as the other two subtypes of Four.

Social Subtype Fours focus more on their deficiencies and also on earning the understanding and appreciation of the groups to which they belong. They want understanding and appreciation for their suffering and sorrows, and desire acknowledgment for their heartfelt contributions to groups, while at the same time they often feel marginal to or not fully part of groups.

One-to-One Subtype Fours feel compelled to express their needs and feelings outwardly and can be highly competitive with others to gain attention, to be heard, and to be acknowledged for their perspectives and accomplishments. Winning is perceived as another venue for being understood, and coming out on top is seen as a way to resolve their continuous comparisons with others.

Wings, Arrows and Subtypes | Enneagram Fives

Wings for Fives

Four Wing: Fives with a Four wing are more emotionally sensitive and expressive and also have an aesthetic perspective, perhaps engaging in the arts themselves – for example, writing poetry, novels, or screenplays and/or being photographers or artists.

Six Wing: Fives with a Six wing emphasize and engage more readily with teams, tend to place greater value on loyalty, and may have enhanced intuitive insight. Although many other Fives can also be quite insightful, their insights come more from putting facts together and engaging in extensive analysis. When Fives have a Six wing, the insights come more quickly as the product of instantaneous processing.

Arrow Lines for Fives

Arrow Line to Seven: Fives with strong access to arrow line Seven can be playful and spontaneous, far more comfortable being in highly visible roles (as if they are actors playing a particular part) and more highly engaged during social interactions.

Arrow Line from Eight: Fives with strong access to arrow line Eight display more depth of personal power, are less hesitant and more risk-taking and courageous, and move to action far more quickly.

Three Subtypes for Fives

All Fives have an intense need to acquire knowledge and wisdom and a similarly strong desire to avoid intrusion and loss of energy, and they guard and preserve everything that they think they will need – for example, information, physical space, emotional privacy, personal energy, and resources. There are three distinct ways in which Fives manifest these characteristics.

Self-Preservation Subtype Fives are primarily concerned with being intruded upon and being overextended physically and energetically. In a sense, they hoard their involvement with others in the same way they hoard their scarce resources.

Social Subtype Fives want to find and develop strong connections with individuals who share their super-ideals, but they become disengaged when forced to live in a way that is not aligned with these higher-order beliefs. They focus on the group in search of extraordinary individuals, then hoard these relationships and/or their shared ideas and, in the Five's view, superior values.

One-to-One Subtype Fives search for a strong, deep connection with one other person whom they can trust and share confidences with, then hoard themselves, the other person, and these special relationships.

Wings, Arrows and Subtypes | Enneagram Sixes

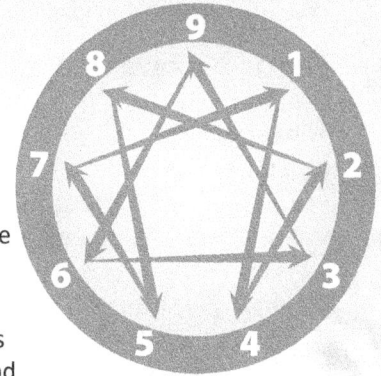

Wings for Sixes

Five Wing: When Sixes have a Five wing, they are more internally than externally focused and are also more self-contained and restrained, thus tempering their tendency to be reactive. In addition, they have an increased passion for knowledge and use the pursuit of knowledge not only to gather information in order to feel prepared, but also for the pure enjoyment of learning.

Seven Wing: It is sometimes said that Sixes see the glass as half empty and Sevens see it as half full. Thus, when Sixes have a Seven wing, they see the whole glass and therefore tend to be more cheerful, less worried, more optimistic, and higher-energy.

Arrow Lines for Sixes

Arrow Line to Three: Sixes with access to Three can bypass their uncertainty by focusing on concrete goals and approaching their work with palpable confidence.

Arrow Line from Nine: Sixes use their connection to Nine to relax, something very helpful to the normally tightly wired Six. For example, taking time to walk or enjoy nature fills Sixes with a feeling of safety and calmness. They are more appreciative of different viewpoints and perspectives, a quality that can be invaluable in times of duress when Sixes start projecting and imagining their perspective as the only viable one.

Three Subtypes for Sixes

All Sixes seek meaning, certainty, and trust, hoping that the best is possible, yet simultaneously fearing that this will not happen, and they doubt that others are trustworthy and/or whether they themselves are capable of meeting the challenges involved. There are three distinct ways in which Sixes manifest these characteristics.

Self-Preservation Subtype Sixes manifest fear as an intense need to feel protected from danger, often seeking the family or a surrogate family to provide this. Self-preservation Sixes also use warmth and friendliness as a way to attract and maintain these types of support groups for the purpose of making themselves feel safe.

Social Subtype Sixes deal with fear by focusing on the rules, regulations, and prescribed ways of behaving within their social environment and organization in an attempt to keep their own behavior in the acceptable range, trying to make sure they do nothing that will cause authority figures to chastise or punish them for going astray.

One-to-One Subtype Sixes are generally the most counter-phobic. They express their fear primarily through the denial of their anxieties and vulnerabilities by pushing against the fear, appearing bold, confident, and sometimes fierce. They can also engage in physical or verbal behavior that makes them feel and appear highly courageous.

Wings, Arrows and Subtypes | Enneagram Sevens

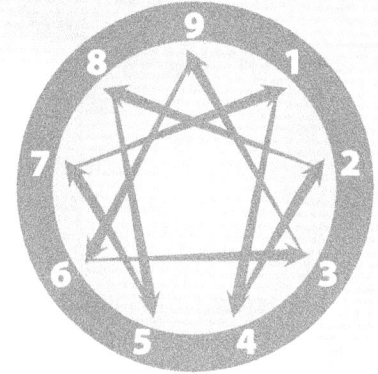

Wings for Sevens

Six Wing: Sevens with a Six wing add the capacity to understand situations as being both half-full and half-empty. Because these Sevens have an increased perceptiveness and an ability to anticipate potential problems, their actions become more deliberate and less based on their instantaneous reactions.

Eight Wing: Sevens with an Eight wing tend to be more direct, assertive, and powerful. They have a more grounded presence and an increased desire to put ideas into action.

Arrow Lines for Sevens

Arrow Line to One: When Sevens have access to arrow line One, their sense of responsibility and ability to focus increases, as does their precision and attention to detail. Although some Sevens use these qualities on an ongoing basis, many display them most often as work deadlines approach.

Arrow Line from Five: Sevens expend vast amounts of energy, and they eventually become fatigued. Access to Five allows them to take time for themselves without engaging with others (although this may last only a few hours every few months). In addition, some Sevens who have an extremely strong link to Five enjoy quietude on a more regular basis, engage in self-reflection more often, and tend to be more self-contained.

Three Subtypes for Sevens

All Sevens have an insatiable thirst for new stimulation of all kinds and distract themselves with interesting people, ideas, and pleasurable experiences, which allows them to avoid their fear of painful emotions and difficult situations. There are three distinct ways in which Sevens manifest these characteristics.

Self-Preservation Subtype Sevens try to create close networks of family, friends, and colleagues, not only to keep themselves feeling both stimulated and secure but also to generate new and interesting opportunities to pursue.

Social Subtype Sevens sacrifice some of their need for stimulation in the service of the group or of some ideal that is extremely important to them. At the same time, they are aware of wanting to pursue their desire for excitement, but they choose to postpone it.

One-to-One Subtype Sevens are dreamers, with a need to see the stark reality of the world through rose-colored glasses, and they are the most optimistic of the three subtypes of type Seven. Often, they become fascinated with one other person, become satiated with that person over time, then find someone new who intrigues and stimulates them.

Wings, Arrows and Subtypes | Enneagram Eights

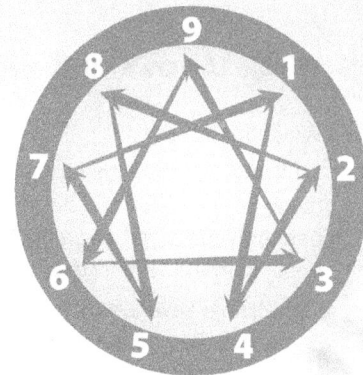

Wings for Eights

Seven Wing: Eights with a Seven wing add a lightheartedness to the usually more serious Eight outlook, are more high-spirited and independent, and tend to be far more adventurous, willing to try new things in their personal and professional lives for the sake of experimentation and enjoyment.

Nine Wing: Eights with a Nine wing are interpersonally warmer, more calm, and less reactive, and they solicit and listen to others' opinions because they are more consensually oriented.

Arrow Lines for Eights

Arrow Line to Five: Eights with a link to Five often use the solitary qualities of Five as a way to recharge themselves after particularly stressful or painful events or after expending their excessive mental, emotional, and physical energy to make big things happen. Eights with an extremely strong connection to Five are often more highly self-reflective than other Eights, and they may engage in intellectual pursuits solely for the pleasure of learning.

Arrow Line from Two: Eights with a strong connection to Two are very warm, generous, and openhearted. They are more gentle than Eights without this link, and they show a deeper level of empathy for others.

Three Subtypes for Eights

As a way to pursue justice and control and to avoid and deny their anxiety and sadness or feelings of vulnerability, Eights engage in a variety of self-satisfying behaviors and do these in an excessive way; for example, they take big and immediate action, work superhuman hours, eat too much food, exercise for three hours a day for a week and then don't exercise for two months, and more. There are three distinct ways in which Eights manifest these characteristics.

Self-Preservation Subtype Eights focus their excessiveness and energy on getting what they need for survival, and they become highly frustrated, intolerant, and angry when the fulfillment of these needs is thwarted. Of the three Eight subtypes, the self-preservation subtype Eights tend to speak the least and to approach situations – particularly those they deem important to their survival – in a highly strategic way that allows them to get the upper hand.

Social Subtype Eights vigorously protect others from unjust and unfair authorities and systems and challenge social norms. At the same time, they seek power, influence, and pleasure. Wanting loyalty from others and being highly loyal themselves, they derive a feeling of power from challenging others as well as from defending those under their protection, which makes them feel less vulnerable.

One-to-One Subtype Eights are the most intense, rebellious, and emotional of the three Eight subtypes. Provocative and passionate in a way that draws others toward them, these Eights derive their power and influence from being at the center of things, from the strong and energetic connections they develop, and from the fervent way in which they express their positions and values.

Wings, Arrows and Subtypes | Enneagram Nines

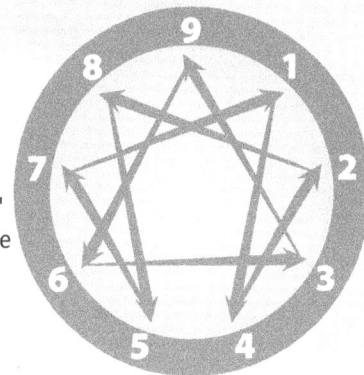

Wings for Nines

Eight Wing: Nines with an Eight wing have a more take-charge orientation, exhibiting a solidity and forcefulness while still maintaining a desire to hear others' opinions. With a very strong Eight wing, Nines assert their own points of view more readily and make fast and clear decisions, even in the face of strong opposition.

One Wing: When Nines have a One wing, they are more attentive – for example, they pay more attention to details and are more punctual and precise. Although Nines often diffuse their attention, a One wing increases their overall focus, acuity, clarity, and discernment.

Arrow Lines for Nines

Arrow Line to Six: When Nines have a strong link to Six, their level of insight about self, others, and situations increases, and they tend to be more deliberative and verbally expressive.

Arrow Line from Three: Nines with a strong connection to Three have a stronger goal focus and results orientation, qualities that help them shift from the distractions of seeking comforting and comfortable activities to a more forward-moving, action-oriented approach to life and work.

Three Subtypes for Nines

In order to maintain harmony and comfort and to avoid conflict, Nines numb themselves to their own reactions by becoming lethargic or by not paying attention to their own deeper feelings, needs, and impulses, thus disabling them from knowing what they think and want and which action is the right one to take. There are three distinct ways in which Nines manifest these characteristics.

Self-Preservation Subtype Nines use the comfort of routine, rhythmic, and pleasant activities as a way of not paying attention to themselves. Using these repetitive activities to distract themselves from more important issues, many self-preservation Nines also acquire collections, and their desire for these objects increases the more they obtain.

Social Subtype Nines work extremely hard on behalf of a group, organization, or cause that they support or belong to as a way of not focusing on themselves. Social subtype Nines are usually very friendly, and their need to feel a part of things is rooted in their underlying feeling of not fitting in. Thus, Nines sacrifice themselves in the service of others, rarely showing the pain, stress, and overwork they experience as a result.

One-to-One Subtype Nines join or merge with others who are important to them as a way of not paying attention to their own thoughts, feelings, and needs. This fusion with others results in One-to-One subtype Nines becoming disconnected from their own deep desires and confusing their own intentions and fulfillment with those of these important others.

ORGANIZATION DEVELOPMENT BOOKS | CONSULTING with THE ENNEAGRAM

Argyris, C. (1993). *Knowledge for Action: A Guide for Overcoming Barriers to Organizational Change*. San Francisco: Jossey-Bass.

Chestnut, B. (2013). *The Complete Enneagram*. Berkeley: She Writes Press.

Block, P. (2000). *Flawless Consulting, 2nd edition*. New York: The Guilford Press.

Bunker, B., and Alban, B. (1997). *Large Group Interventions: Engaging the Whole System for Rapid Change*. San Francisco: Jossey-Bass.

Cooperrider, D. L., Sorensen, P. F., Yaeger, T. F., and Whitney, D., editors (2001). *Appreciative Inquiry: An Emerging Direction for Organization Development*. Champaign: Stipes Publishing.

French, W. L., Bell, C. H., Jr., and Zawack, R. A. (2000). *Organization Development: Theory, Practice, and Research*. Dallas: Business Publications.

Galbraith, J. R., Downey, D., and Kates, A. (2002). *Designing Dynamic Organizations*. New York: AMACOM.

Galbraith, J. R. (1995). *Designing Organizations: An Executive Briefing on Strategy, Structure, and Process*. San Francisco: Jossey-Bass.

Galbraith, J. R., Lawler III, E. E., and Associates (1993). *Organizing for the Future: The New Logic for Managing Complex Organizations*. San Francisco: Jossey-Bass.

Gladwell, M. (2000). *The Tipping Point*. New York: Little, Brown & Company.

Kim, W. C., and Mauborgne, R. (2005). *Blue Ocean Strategy: How to Create Uncontested Market Space and Make the Competition Irrelevant*. Boston: Harvard Business School Press.

Kotter, J. P. (1996). *Leading Change*. Boston: Harvard Business School Press.

Lapid-Bogda, G. (2010). *Bringing Out the Best in Everyone You Coach*. New York: McGraw-Hill.

Lapid-Bogda, G. (2004). *Bringing Out the Best in Yourself at Work*. New York: McGraw-Hill.

Lapid-Bogda, G. (2013). *Know Your Type*, the comprehensive Enneagram mobile app. Available on the Apple App Store, and Amazon Appstore.

Lapid-Bogda, G. (2011). *The Enneagram Development Guide, 2nd edition*. Santa Monica: The Enneagram In Business Press.

Lapid-Bogda, G. (2007). *What Type of Leader Are You?* New York: McGraw-Hill.

Lippitt, G. L., and Lippitt, R. (1986). *The Consulting Process in Action*. San Diego: Pfeiffer & Co.

Maister, D. H. (1993). *Managing the Professional Service Firm*. New York: Free Press.

Maister, D. H. (2003). *Practice What You Preach*. New York: Free Press.

Maister, D. H. (1997). *True Professionalism: The Courage to Care About Your People, Your Clients, and Your Career*. New York: Free Press.

Maister, D. H., Green, C. H., and Galford, R. M. (2000). *The Trusted Advisor*. New York: Touchstone.

Maitri, S. (2001). *The Spiritual Dimension of the Enneagram: Nine Faces of the Soul*. New York: Tarcher/Putnam.

Massarik, F., and Pei-Carpenter, M. (2002). *Organization Development and Consulting: Perspectives and Foundations*. San Francisco: Jossey-Bass/Pfeiffer.

McKenna, P. J., and Maister, D. H. (2002). *First Among Equals: How to Manage a Group of Professionals*. New York: Free Press.

Nadler, D. A., Gerstein, M. S., Shaw, R. B., and Associates (1992). *Organizational Architecture: Designs for Changing Organizations*. San Francisco: Jossey-Bass.

Naranjo, C. (2003). *Character and Neurosis: An Integrative View, 4th edition*. Nevada City: Gateways/IDHHB, Inc.

Oshry, B. I. (1999). *Leading Systems: Lessons from the Power Lab*. San Francisco: Berrett-Koehler.

Reddy, W. B. (1994). *Intervention Skills: Process Consultation for Small Groups and Teams*. San Diego: Pheiffer & Co.

Robinson, D. G., and Robinson, J. C. (2005). *Strategic Business Partner: Aligning People Strategies with Business Goals*. San Francisco: Berrett-Koehler.

Schein, E. (1999). *The Corporate Culture Survival Guide*. San Francisco: Jossey-Bass.

Senge, P. M. (1990). *The Fifth Discipline: The Art and Practice of the Learning Organization*. New York: Doubleday Currency.

Senge, P. M., Kleiner, A., Roberts, C., Ross, R. B., and Smith, B. J. (1994). *The Fifth Discipline Fieldbook: Strategies and Tools for Building a Learning Organization*. New York: Doubleday Currency.

Smith, K. K., and Berg, D. N. (1987). *Paradoxes of Group Life*. San Francisco: Jossey-Bass.

Trompenaars, F. (1993). *Riding the Waves of Culture: Understanding Cultural Diversity in Business*. London: The Economist Books.

Ulrich, D., and Ulrich, W. (2010). *The Why of Work*. New York: McGraw-Hill.

Van der Heijden, K. (1996). *Scenarios: The Art of Strategic Conversation*. Chichester: John Wiley & Sons.

Weisbord, M. R. (1992). *Discovering Common Ground*. San Francisco: Berrett-Koehler.

Weisbord, M. R. (1978). *Organizational Diagnosis: A Workbook of Theory and Practice*. Reading: Addison-Wesley.

Weisbord, M. R. (1987). *Productive Workplaces: Organizing and Managing for Dignity, Meaning, and Community*. San Francisco: Jossey-Bass.

ABOUT THE AUTHOR

Ginger Lapid-Bogda PhD | Enneagram author and teacher, as well as an organization development consultant, trainer and coach, Ginger works with organizations, leaders, and teams around the globe to create vibrant, productive, and sustainable organizations. Author of five Enneagram-business books, she also offers global certification programs that enable consultants, trainers, and coaches to use the Enneagram effectively and accurately in organizational applications such as teams, leadership, conflict, feedback, strategy, organizational change and transformation, and personal and professional development.

In addition, Ginger has created abundant resources for individuals and organizations that make the Enneagram more accessible and easy-to-use without compromising the integrity of this powerful system. Some of the resources include: Train-the-Trainer programs based on *Bringing Out the Best in Yourself at Work* and *What Type of Leader Are You?*; two ICF ACSTH coaching programs, Coaching with the Enneagram and Advanced Coaching with the Enneagram, both based on *Bringing Out the Best in Everyone You Coach*; a dynamic consulting skills program based on *Consulting with the Enneagram*; 25+ full-color training tools that jump-start Enneagram training programs; *Know Your Type*, the Enneagram App; a subscription-based Enneagram eLearning Portal; and a worldwide network of Enneagram professionals (Enneagram in Business Network) that provides best-in-class Enneagram training, coaching and consulting, both globally and locally.

Ginger has been consulting with Fortune 500 and non-profit organizations for over 35 years, and she currently works with companies such as Genentech/ Roche, Salesforce.com, Nestle, among others.

Ginger's books
Bringing Out the Best in Yourself at Work (2004) | core work applications of the Enneagram
What Type of Leader Are You? (2007) | leadership competencies using the Enneagram
Bringing Out the Best in Everyone You Coach (2010) | high-impact coaching using the Enneagram
The Enneagram Development Guide (2011) | 50+ powerful development activities for each Enneagram style
Consulting with the Enneagram (2015) | a systematic structure for achieving powerful results with clients

TheEnneagramInBusiness.com | a highly informational and well-organized site providing Enneagram and business concepts and practices from around the world, plus consulting, training, and coaching services, as well as schedules of public certification programs| info@theenneagraminbusiness.com

www.ingramcontent.com/pod-product-compliance
Lightning Source LLC
Chambersburg PA
CBHW080516090426
42734CB00015B/3069

9 780692 412695